Janet's unique personality is her
my life and getting the results I s
list of things Janet tells me to do
work we do surrounding improving my relationship w... ..,
platform, I create the power and confidence to dream, execute and achieve. That is the gift.

~ *Joe Romano, Sicilianaire, comedian and chef (San Francisco)*

"21 Days to Yes!" is a life-changing experience. I am amazed at my results of 80% increased productivity and ownership, 50% increased communication effectiveness and an overall sense of freedom. Although I did the work in this self-investing program, Janet Caliri has been with me, providing structure, objective clarity and support. In just 21 days, I am now aligned with my purpose, grounded in my power, and laser focused in a way I have yearned for but never quite demonstrated. Janet is a gifted life coach who lives her purpose of inspiring the potential of others. I highly recommend Janet and her "21 Days to Yes!" program to anyone motivated and willing to step up and claim a life of ownership for themselves.

~ *Rob R. Dunn, Real estate investor (Nampa, Idaho)*

Ownership is an approach in taking personal responsibility for my actions, words, emotions and behavior. I then make choices that are conscious and compassionate and look to myself for the answers that I seek. I rely on the inherent inner strength, guidance and wisdom I possess. The unique vision and perspective I have in life is *valuable* and *worthy* of being expressed in my deepest truth, moment to moment as a gift to myself and the world. Through working with Janet Caliri, she encouraged a high level of ownership from and for me. In turn, I began to choose the route of taking responsibility in areas of my life where it was lacking. As a result, I have come to realize that I am a *capable human being*. When I own my situations, behavior and choices, I am living in my power. I am grateful to Janet for her guidance in this area!

~ *Aisha Kabia, Actress (Los Angeles)*

Janet Caliri's coaching work combines the creativity and perceptivity of an artist with the compassion, persistence and dedication of a caring guide and friend. Her unique method of visually aided coaching has helped me to see myself more clearly and honestly inside and out. With her help, I have found a career in which I can express both my creative and logical sides as well my desires to grow personally while helping others do the same. If a picture is worth a thousand words, Janet's work and pictures are worth a thousand self-help books.

~ *Jay Smith, Assoc. Professor,*
Inamori Academy of Management & Technology, Kagoshima University

I have had the blessings and good fortune of coaching with Janet. This process has been priceless and I wake up with a whole different feeling now. Her ethics, her wisdom, her discipline, her caring, her follow-through, her guidance . . . are outstanding. I highly recommend her work only if you are ready to transform and only if you are ready to grow into your potential! Janet will guide you there. Gift yourself with this amazing opportunity . . . before she is too booked up.

~ *Ortalia Rogers*
World-renowned psychic, healer, metaphysical teacher
and leader of sacred global journeys (Brooklyn, NY)

As a successful entrepreneur, having a life coach truly changed my perspective on my world. I never considered myself a person that would benefit from knowing me better. Working with Janet showed me there was so much more potential locked up inside waiting to be unleashed towards a more successful me. I stand as a true believer in the power of Janet's teachings and the subsequent benefits, such as:

- ☼ I am more successful in relationships with myself and with others (90% increase).
- ☼ I am more assertive in my entrepreneurial spirit (43% increase in productivity).
- ☼ I am more compassionate (200% increase).
- ☼ I am a more effective communicator (42% increase).
- ☼ I determined and actualized and remain in my purpose.
- ☼ I am more "me" than before.

I recommend Janet Caliri, and even more so the "21 Days to Yes!" program, to anyone who sees capturing the power of their potential as an investment for their present and their future.

~ *Keith Alyea, Principal, Market Reform (Charlotte, NC)*

Prior to working with Janet in her Law of Attraction class, I was a person full of potential but unaware as to how to maximize it. Working with Janet has transformed my life. I now choose to honor my talents and my gifts in ways that not only enhance what I desire but simultaneously inspire others to reach their potential as well. Since working with Janet I have signed with an agent, generated more income and organized my life to easily achieve my goals and dreams. I recommend Janet because she is not only a life coach, she is an inspiration.

~ *Sandy Bowles, Actress (Los Angeles)*

Me with Me

**"I am as good to others
to the degree I am with me."**

Janet Caliri

© 2008 Janet Caliri
All Rights Reserved

No part of this book may be reproduced or utilized in any form
or by any electronic means without written permission from the author.

Cover art by Melinda Hannah

Cover and interior design and editing by Backspace Ink

ISBN-10: 1-44046-547-9
ISBN-13: 978-1-44046-547-5

Mom,
I dedicate this book to you, my generous Mother,
Catherine "Sis" Caliri

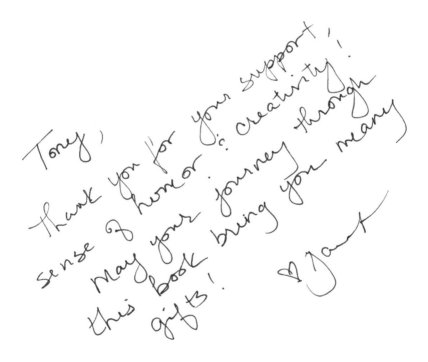

Tony,
Thank you for your support, sense of humor & creativity!
May your journey through this book bring you many gifts!
♥ Janet

Contents

A Note About a Higher Power 11

Acknowledgements 12

Preface 14

Introduction 18
Exercise: What I Like About Myself 19

Chapter One. A Few Words About Coaching 21
What Is a Coach? 21
What Is the Purpose of Coaching? 22

Chapter Two. Change 24
Exercise: The Keys to Freedom, Joy and Bliss 25
Exercise: Value Statistic Barometer—Stage 1 26
Does Change Have a Bad Rap? 27
∞ *Dream or Comfort?* 28
Exercise: Step 1—Want 29
Exercise: Step 2—Desire 29
Believe 31
Exercise: Step 3—Commit 31
∞ *Making a Deal with God* 32
The Secret of Believing 33
Want—Desire—Commit 33
Self-compassion 34
Three Steps Toward Self-compassion 35
Taking a Good Look 35

∞ *"I'm Doing What I Want to Do!"* 36
Intention 37
Intention—Invention 37
Gratitude 38
∞ *"A" Student* 38
∞ *"Back Off! I'm Beating Myself Up!"* 39
∞ *Grumpy Curmudgeon or Gracious Champion? by Jim* 40
Self-respect 41
∞ *Self-respect* 41
∞ *Beth with Beth by Beth* 42
∞ *The Best* 43
Communication Model 45
∞ *Communication Model and a Lesson in Nonattachment* 46
Exercise: Communicate Effectively 47

Chapter Three. Ownership **48**
Claim It! 48
∞ *Thoughtful Achiever* 49
∞ *An Effective Path to Peace* 50
Ownership is Freedom 50
∞ *Waxing the Car* 51
The Miracle of Ownership: How I Overcame Depression 53
Choice 54
∞ *One Simple Choice by Alisha* 55
Exercise: I Have Choice in Every Moment 55
∞ *To the Rescue! by Ortalia* 56
Law of Attraction 57
∞ *Entitled Daughter* 59
Manifestation 59
∞ *Unintentional Envisioning* 59
∞ *Authority Issues Anonymous* 60
Integrity 61
Being Bigger Than My Reasons 62
∞ *I Should* 63
Exercise: Keeping My Word with Ease (Step 1) 64

Chapter Four. The Gift of Thoughts and Words **66**
New Thought Leads to New Results 66

CONTENTS

What I Focus on, I Get 67
∞ *Prisoner of Unhealthy Thoughts* 67
Exercise: Experimenting with Words 68
Say "I" 69
You Make Me 70
I Am 71
Exercise: Flip Side 72

Chapter Five. Raising My Consciousness 74
Know Thyself 74
Sixth Sense 74
∞ *Trusting My Gut* 75
Exercise: Preparatory Questions 76
Intuition: The Rite of Passage 78
Paranoia 79
Exercise: Practical Head or Intuitive Gut? 80
∞ *Red Flag Raisin Time!* 81
JUMP: Joyful Unlimited Manifesting Potential 83
Embracing Our Differences 83
How to Get Past My Differences 84
∞ *Unstoppable* 85
Exercise: Getting Past My Differences 85
Triggers 86
Position Release 87
Exercise: Self-criticism 88
∞ *I Grow in the Presence of Janet Caliri by Noel* 89
Exercise: Value Statistic Barometer—Stage 2 90

Chapter Six. Purpose 93
Without Purpose, What's the Point? 93
Exercise: A Reason to Get Out of Bed 94
Vehicles for Purpose 96
∞ *A Well That Never Runs Dry by Yael* 96
Mastering My Mojo 98
Exercise: Determine My Mojo 99
Core "Juicy" Experiences 101
Exercise: Determine Core Juicy Experiences 102
∞ *Attention, Please!* 103

Memorize, Internalize, Actualize 104
∞ *The Passionate Brother, Friend, Father, Son and Husband* 105
Self-acknowledgement 105
Creative, Full Self-expression 106
Exercise: Who Am I? 107
Exercise: Keeping My Word with Ease (Step 2) 108

Chapter Seven. Evolution 111
Momentum 111
Forgiveness 113
∞ *Simply Committing to Forgive* 113
Antidotes for Successful Forgiveness 114
∞ *Thoughts on Forgiveness by Camille* 114
∞ *Blue Line–Green Line Greed* 116

Chapter Eight. Review 118
New Results 118
Surrounding Myself with Like-minded People 119
Leadership Support 119
Potential 120
Exercise: Value Statistic Barometer—Stage 3 122

Appendix A. Coaching Services and Information 124

Appendix B. Links for More Information 126

Glossary 128

About the Author 136
The Vision Behind Sight for Sound 136

A Note About a Higher Power

Dear Readers:

My purpose is to ignite your potential. When I speak about a Higher Power in this book, I do not assume that you believe in one. I know that you all come from different walks of life.

You are not required to believe in a Higher Power in order to create magnificent results from my techniques. What is required is a desire, however small, to play around with what is possible, knowing that you have choice and are not locked into anything.

If it appears that believing in a Higher Power is necessary, know that it is not. *Life is an experiment.*

Experimentation requires a degree—perhaps the smallest inkling—of trust and faith in oneself. There are those who enjoy having a Higher Power to strengthen their own inherent trust and faith; I happen to be one of them.

Acknowledgements

Mom and Dad: Thank you for putting aside your judgments and remaining committed to my greatness, whether or not we agree on what that looks like or how it "should" be. Your belief in me is astonishing.

Christine, Billy, Derek (Derky), Alexa (Pookie), Tristan (Bubba), Frank, Cass, Sedona, Mark, Amy, Samantha, Alexandra and the newest addition, Max: Simply with your presence, I have become a better woman, sister, friend, aunt and confidante.

To the rest of my amazing family unit: I love you so much! Thank you for the many happy times. We shall always stick together.

Gary, a temporary mirror for relentlessly revealing everything that was holding me back, tearing down my walls and slapping me awake: You knew what your purpose was with me, and you stayed tried and true to opening my eyes to the universe and a higher being other than myself. I am truly grateful and indebted to you forever. Reflecting back has allowed me to understand the true meaning of relationships. They are not to capture and hold the other, or necessarily to last a long time; they are to remind me of who I am and where I desire to go as a higher spiritual being in this lifetime.

Roberto: You encouraged my free spirit and full self-expression, although I didn't know it or appreciate it then. You are a lifelong gift to me whom I cherish, though you have been thousands and thousand of miles away. You are my soul mate.

Homey: I always felt laid back in your presence. You opened my eyes to taking life less seriously and being detached from all things. Thank you for connecting with me from the other side.

ACKNOWLEDGEMENTS

Jackie, my soul mate, my godmother, my mirror: We needn't say a word to each other; we just knew. I still "know" and realize that connection with you on the other side.

Christopher: You remind me to be patient and faithful of my passionate visions.

Judy and the late Randy Revell, Elisabeth, Lori and Phil: How blessed I am to know you and participate in your mission so closely and experientially.

Alejandra: You are the space for me to be vulnerable without negative judgment; to be the student without shame and a reminder of my feminine energy.

To my Sisterhood, my Family Sunday Dinner community, Context Associated, Extraordinary Learning, Mentors and Friends all over the world: You know who you are.

To Kari and Frank: Your preliminary editing and feedback was the catalyst for me to continue moving forward in making this real.

Joanne, "Editor Extraordinaire": Your spirit, individualism, creativity, patience and organization are the perfect ingredients in making this real! I'm so glad I followed my intuition in choosing you!

To my "Ghost Readers": Your dedication and feedback is notably instrumental in the value of this book. Thank you so much for taking on the task!

To those whose personal stories are told throughout this book: Thank you for your willingness to share.

Finally, to each and every client: I want you to know what an incredible teacher you are for me.

Preface

Many of my personal experiences—as well as those of friends, family and clients—have inspired this book. The truth that evolution (change) is a journey . . . never ending and eternal . . . is exciting to me. When I began looking at change as world truth, I saw it as an opportunity rather than an obligation or something I should resist.

I didn't masturbate until I was 35 years old, which is also when I had my first orgasm. When I was a kid, I stuttered and was assigned to a learning disability class for what seemed like forever but was only a few years. I sucked my thumb until I was 11 years old. My mother slowly cut away the blanket I used until there was nothing left, just so she wouldn't shock me.

The kids in my Boston suburban neighborhood used to ask, "What flavor is it, Janet? Chocolate or vanilla?"

One time, I answered, "Orange sherbet," because that was my favorite flavor.

When I was 24 years old, I intuitively decided that stepping into all of my fears was going to dissolve or reduce them. From that moment on, I jumped:

JUMP = Joyful Unlimited Manifesting Potential

I became courageously independent. While those are great qualities, I reminded myself to remain open to what life is offering me, such as love, romance and partnership, and to contribute in a way that is so big—bigger than I can imagine—with the potential that naturally comes with discomfort.

In 2000, I felt stuck, as if I knew there was something more, something that I was not being. It was time for Joyful Unlimited Manifesting Potential. I

PREFACE

knew that getting good with me was how I got good with others. I realized that, when I am giving to myself, I am giving to others.

Over a period of time, I had invited friends and family to take a road trip across the country with me. In these years, most of my friends and family were in serious relationships, getting married or having babies, so I went myself. Driving my 11-year-old car, packed with sufficient goods, $650 and no credit card, I was on my way.

I am blessed to have many friends, and many who live around the United States, so I planned my path with time to visit them. Other than that, I stayed in a couple of hotels and hostels, which are always interesting experiences.

I had never been to California. I said for years that I would never live there because of the earthquakes and the ground sinking into the ocean; yet, when I arrived in San Francisco, I felt a magic that is indescribable. I spent exactly 24 hours there and headed back east. As I drove away, I cried for two hours and, at some point, called my sister, pleading, "I don't want to leave San Francisco!" During my trek back east, I made the choice to move to that magical city one year later.

I completed projects with my photography business, saved some money and organized a truck to haul my stuff across the country. In the meantime, I looked for jobs in the photography industry, flying back out for interviews with magazines and newspapers. It seemed that there were very few opportunities there for a professional photographer, so I surrendered control of what was supposed to show up and happen for me. I jumped.

I looked through Craigslist and found an ad from two founders of a leadership company, stating their mission to strengthen the fabric of goodwill. They were looking for an assistant and companion for Judy, the cofounder who was in a wheelchair, and explained that the position included traveling with them to their leadership seminars. I thought, "Wow, 'strengthening the fabric of goodwill' is very aligned with who I am, and this seems like an opportunity for me to surround myself with like-minded people."

I applied for the job, was scheduled for an interview, flew back out there from Boston and was hired the day after my interview. I had exactly one month to get my stuff together, give away my belongings, pack and start anew in an uncharted territory. I was energized and felt very good about it. I *knew* it was the best decision for me despite what others thought or how close I was to my family.

I headed out west and landed there on July 1st, and moved into my little guest suite in the home of Judy and Randy Revell, the founders of Context Associated. I loved breathing in the air filled with eucalyptus, and experiencing the new sights and sounds, the people energy, the music and a fresh openness to self-expression.

I continued to run my freelance photography business simultaneously, having the opportunity to work with the San Francisco Academy for Performing Arts and other creative artists. After two years of working with Judy and Randy, meeting their family and creating my own family through developing friendships with graduates of their programs and acquaintances, I moved to Los Angeles to incorporate television and film into my photography business.

I moved with two "friends" and, a few months later, fled the house and found myself homeless. At that point, I developed a monthly Leadership Circle, inspiring every person I knew to live in their potential and become leaders in their own life, while surrounding myself with like-minded people.

All the while, Randy said, "Janet, there's something missing with your photography business, your career. You are the power behind the throne and people 'stick' to you."

I concurred, and committed myself to being open to what my new career looked like, yet I had no clue. Two weeks later, I had an epiphany: become a life coach and incorporate photography to document that what's on the inside shows up on the outside. I started taking before-and-after photos of my clients to demonstrate their new essence by way of knowing themselves better.

In the spring of 2005, I jumped and got engaged; a few months later, he changed his mind. I now consider the breakup a breakdown and a powerful breakthrough about telling myself the truth. Up until then, I was living in the future potential of men (and women). The time of living my life with enthusiasm, and knowing its potential, was breaking through at any moment, so it was okay for me to give up my values in the process of that dazzling dream. I ignored the red flags because I was so committed to those people and their potential.

Two months later, I revisited my favorite transformational course, "21st Century Leadership," and declared that "Janet with Janet" was the best place for me to be in that moment and forever.

Selling my soul was not going to create the positive results that I desired, but selling my soul unconsciously was certainly creating the "juice." Those results felt awesome in the moment, but they were being met destructively.

My end result: Everything fell from beneath me. I was ungrounded, uncertain and ashamed—and devastated.

The day after the breakup, I called my brother Frank from a family-owned hotel somewhere in Vancouver, B.C. I remember saying, "Who the hell am I to be a coach . . . to be teaching others leadership and ownership?"

Frank compassionately replied, "Janet, you are human. Knowing you and how courageous you are, you will be a positive model for your clients in how you positively respond, behave and prosper through this difficult phase of your life."

I then spent three months with my family in Boston making lemonade out of lemons. I acquired a few new clients through leading workshops, and became closer with my family.

I had major trepidations going to Boston and asking my family to help me through this troublesome time. They were the last people from whom I wanted help; however, as soon as I arrived, I shared how I prefer to be helped and, in agreement, surrendered to their assistance by putting aside my shame and stubbornness. I listened. I listened well. I opened my heart and mind to anything they were willing to give in moving forward with a sense of pride, value, respect and self-love. I hired an amazing business coach named Heather Brodie.

I let myself grieve for as long as necessary, stayed out of "victim mode" and made this an opportunity of a lifetime. Indeed, it was then and it still is. I bless my ex-fiancé and wish him the best in life. I thank God frequently for what occurred then, and everything that occurred thereafter, for a new door opened to be with my true love.

In the following pages, I share some of my personal stories and experiences (and some from others) with the goal of providing solace and inspiration. I encourage you to live in your potential, safely and shamelessly, with unwavering full self-expression and without guilt.

Introduction

> For simplicity, this book is written primarily in the first person and present tense to assist you, my audience, in absorbing the pages with a greater probability of internalizing the teachings—through the "I" (owning it) present tense and through relating to the personal experiences, thereby allowing yourself to live in your potential.

I am truly grateful for the freedom of full self-expression. Most of us are hesitant to fully express ourselves for fear of negative consequences, such as the responsibility that comes along with our power or the possibility of being shunned by others. Being unattached to the outcome is something to exercise and believe in if we desire enlightenment.

This book is a vehicle to ignite your potential and assist you in remembering who you are and realizing your purpose here on Planet Earth. Your own experiences will bring you to this place of falling in love with yourself more deeply. You are as good to others to the degree you are with yourself ... with an overflow of passion for giving and loving deeply.

> My life purpose is igniting human potential. I believe in your potential until you do.

In this book, I include personal stories from people just like you who decided that doing the same thing over and over again only gave the same result. They were ready to make a change, and the results significantly changed the way they now think about themselves and the outcome of their future decisions. The purpose of these stories is to reaffirm that *you can be and do anything you choose.*

INTRODUCTION

> **EXERCISE:**
> ## What I Like About Myself
>
> Grab a piece of paper, notebook, journal, Post-it note or a blank greeting card. You may also use the blank pages in back of this book.
>
> Ask yourself, "What do I like, love and enjoy about myself?" These traits may be in any area such as physical body, personality, career, strengths and hobbies. Recalling compliments you receive may be helpful in deriving the answers. If you drift into areas of self-criticism, stop and redirect yourself to the flip side. For example, "I don't like my body" can be changed to "The *parts* of my body that I do like are_____."
>
> ....
> ....
> ....
> ....
> ....
> ....
> ....
> ....
> ....
> ....

You may choose to read this entire book and then go back to the exercises, or do each exercise along the way. My suggestion is to use this as a reference in your daily life. Whatever you choose, I encourage you to have fun and experiment!

This book is a gift of self-awareness and, with that, you may feel stopped or uncomfortable as you come upon the exercises or strongly disagree with a personal story or teaching. There is no right/wrong, good/bad—only your truth. The fact that you are reading this book says that you are open to loving yourself more deeply.

You can be an unstoppable force and ease back into the book with these six simple steps:
1. Take a few deep breaths.
2. Choose to be compassionate with myself.
3. Forgive myself for the past.
4. Embrace my current thoughts and feelings.
5. Remember that everything is temporary.
6. Recall what I like about myself.

When I see things as they truly are, I make sound choices. When I am giving to myself, I am giving to others. When I nurture myself by making choices of the highest good, it becomes natural without effort. As a result, my productivity increases and I have more energy, desire and time to contribute to others.

I believe that people want to support others, yet putting others first on a consistent basis results in depression, disease and physical ailments due to frustration, resentment, fatigue, lack of focus and imbalance.

Notice what happens as you begin to put yourself first without guilt. An example is making coffee in the morning, which is a process I enjoy. When I allow this to be interrupted by putting something or someone else first, I usually feel irritated and unanchored in my day. When I continue to put myself last over a period of time, I haven't much left over to give to others.

> Put your oxygen mask on first before assisting others.

During take-off in a plane, the flight attendant demonstrates the safety features in case of an emergency. One procedure is regarding the oxygen masks. Do you know why they suggest putting the oxygen mask on you first before assisting others? It is precisely the message of this book. How could you possibly be coherent and rational enough to assist another person when you are not breathing enough oxygen yourself?

CHAPTER ONE

A Few Words About Coaching

WHAT IS A COACH?

A coach is someone who tells you what you don't want to hear, and has you see what you don't want to see, so you can be who you have always known you could be. A coach ignites your potential in ways you think are impossible and never dare imagine. A coach is a human mirror, with similar life experiences as yours, yet is objective, creative, intuitive, confidential and compassionate—one who guides you to see who you truly are.

When you begin to *see* your core essence and determine your purpose, you make *sound* choices. Let the fun begin! In the coaching process, primarily through questioning and listening, the coach assists you in having breakthroughs—big or small, professional or personal—and urges you unfailingly toward insight of your greatness as well as your road blocks. You now get out of your own way and begin creating an effective path and approach to life.

A coach . . .

. . . is not a therapist, an advisor or a counselor.

. . . has a myriad of life experiences upon which to recall and shed light on your situation, turning obligation into opportunity, hopelessness into possibility, victim mentality into freedom (ownership), ugliness into beauty, suffering into joyful contribution and vision into actualization.

. . . is a fallible individual who believes in you and your value, and sees your beauty and spirit on a level that is incomprehensible to most.

. . . is one who stops at nothing to make a difference in your life, ensuring your positive impact on the world.

. . . is sometimes a quirky character who knows you better than you do, from a place of integrity, calling you on your stuff and nurturing you to surrender to your truth.

. . . interweaves skills of intuition and knowledge to question who you are being before asking what actions you are taking.

. . . is willing to put aside a prepared format session, breathe and go for your core, peeling layers one at a time until you come to clarity in that moment.

The foundation of my teaching is ownership and choice under the umbrella of the client's life purpose. I am your mirror, supporting you in raising your consciousness by asking questions; teaching life skills and key concepts; helping you to turn unhealthy patterns, habits and mindsets into healthy ones to make the wisest and healthiest choices for your higher good. I believe we are on this earth to contribute our unique gifts. *You* are the gift!

My clients are strongly encouraged to stay connected with me regularly through e-mail (in between sessions) as a powerful strategy to build confidence, maintain direction and gain a high level of accountability.

WHAT IS THE PURPOSE OF COACHING?

Coaching is a self-investing process in which we work together in a fun, confidential and nonjudgmental relationship in direct alignment with trust and respect. It is results-based and forward-moving. As my client, the return on your investment is proportionate to what you invest in the process. Being self-sufficient is the key to growth opportunity; therefore, you are ultimately responsible for your own results.

Whether you work with a coach on a professional, personal or spiritual level, you are guaranteed a higher level of self-awareness overflowing into every aspect of your life. This is great news simply because the more you know yourself, the better your life works.

The following enhanced results are what you create but to which you are not limited:

- ☼ Increased productivity and confidence
- ☼ Effective communication skills
- ☼ Higher level of commitment and ownership
- ☼ Healthier relationships
- ☼ Balance
- ☼ Compassion for self and for others

A FEW WORDS ABOUT COACHING

☼ A greater sense of joy and gratitude
☼ Clarity of your purpose

With coaching, you reveal on the outside what was temporarily stifled on the inside. You are now unreasonable (beyond normal limits); enraged with excitement and enthusiasm; engaged in possibility; unsurpassed in your purpose, skills, qualities, strengths and commitment to a healthy, wealthy and ecstatic life.

Thank you for being a manifestation of my life purpose!

CHAPTER TWO

Change

**How many coaches does it take to change a light bulb?
Just *one*, but the light bulb must be willing to change!**

A friend of mine shared the above joke with me. I think it's funny and speaks volumes in terms of my approach in supporting others to change.

In Chapter One, you were introduced to the purpose of coaching. Similar to building your muscles at the gym, repetition is critical to gain the benefits. In this chapter, I'll share how to incorporate that for effective change.

I will repeat the following over and over again throughout this book in many different ways:

Giving to me first is a selfless act of love.

Make the change, now. Ask yourself questions like:
- ☼ "What is the healthiest choice for me right now?"
- ☼ "What is most important: resting or giving a helping hand to my daughter?"
- ☼ "Which do I feel: obligated or excited to say 'yes'?"

Every day, repeat over and over again:

Me with Me

_____ **with** _____

(fill in both blanks with your first name)

EXERCISE:

The Keys to Freedom, Joy and Bliss

1. Experiment with relinquishing the following words from your vocabulary: can, can't, able, unable, have to, should, try, because, sorry, but, want, right, wrong, makes me, don't, against, need, supposed to.
2. Speak in the first person ("I") and use the present tense: "now," "today," "in this moment," "I am" versus "I will."
3. Use realities instead of hypotheticals: "I am" versus "What if."
4. Give to yourself first so that you have more to give to others.
5. What's on the inside shows up on the outside. Take a photo of yourself today (a "before" photo) and another photo when you have completed most or all of these techniques (an "after" photo). I recommend being patient and reassessing your life three to six months from now, which may be the best time for your "after" photo.

Today's Date: _____	Completion Date: _____
(insert "before" photo here)	(insert "after" photo here)

EXERCISE:
Value Statistic Barometer—Stage 1

Before delving deeply into this book, I suggest you fill out the table below as follows: In the "Stage 1 Date" column, write down today's date. Rate yourself using a number from "1" to "10" (with "1" being the least and "10" being the greatest level of satisfaction). Ideally, write down the first number that comes to your mind. This rating is inclusive of both your personal and your professional life as it is today. These are tangible, measurable results on which to reflect. Then, in Chapter Five (page 90), you'll be asked to fill in the same table and then, in Chapter Eight (page 122). You will notice a change!

Value Statistic Barometer: Stage 1			
Result	Stage 1 Date _____	Stage 2 Date _____	Stage 3 Date _____
Productivity (energy level, financial gain)			
Accountability/ownership (using ownership words, keeping my word, owning my results)			
Confidence			
Compassion (for myself and others)			
Focus (start, completion, intention, being in the moment)			

(continued on next page)

EXERCISE:
Value Statistic Barometer—Stage 1 *(continued)*

Result			
Clarity of purpose (Do I know my purpose? Am I on purpose regularly?)			
Commitment (to what I say is most important to me)			
Relationships (to myself and others)			
Communication effectiveness (communication model, intention, listening)			
Balance (Am I doing more of what I love to do?)			

DOES CHANGE HAVE A BAD RAP?

Change is inevitable. Change has a bad rap. Discomfort is always present but, without evolution, we as a universal whole would not exist. The level of discomfort I experience is up to me, depending upon how I am being in the change.

I have been clever at avoiding changes in my career, living quarters, automobiles, relationships, spiritual practice, eating habits, attitude and health. I resisted change because of the discomfort. It wasn't the change in and of itself; it was the agony, uneasiness and displeasure I felt that was included with the package. The avoidance caught up with me and manifested in ways I do not care to revisit, but I will . . . I am.

The first step toward change occurred when I looked straight into the mirror and said, "Hello, I'd like something different!"

I now look at change as an experiment. It's temporary, as is everything on this earth. There is nothing permanent. Knowing this, I feel a surge of comfort, like a big hug. In my opinion, change no longer has a bad rap; I welcome it like a warm chocolate chip cookie going down my throat.

I haven't always welcomed change. I was one of those people who clearly avoided it. I know now it was because I did not have access to the tools or techniques to deal with this basic life skill. Now I have it, after capitalizing on infinite teachings.

If I desire a different result, I must do or think differently; if I desire to move forward in my life, I must get off the fence and make a decision. I get off the fence first, and then make a choice. When I vacillate in indecision, my energy remains stuck, like skidding tires in a snow bank with no forward or backward movement.

It is my experience that people are more willing to change their mindset or behavior when they are clear on their intention and realize that a different result is most important *now*.

Here are some steps I use to manifest my desired results:
- ☼ Commit to creating what I say is most important.
- ☼ Have a willingness to be uncomfortable.
- ☼ Surround myself with supportive and positive people.
- ☼ Use a different approach or strategy accordingly.

∞

Dream or Comfort?

I was tutoring a high school student who feared what others thought of her if she asked questions in class. She unconsciously decided that her comfort was more important than learning algebra and, as a result, she became very confused and her grades declined quickly.

I led her through the steps of change with an umbrella focus on the "prize" (the dream result). We then went through a series of questions:
- ☼ What is most important: being comfortable (everyone likes me) or graduating high school for acceptance into cosmetology school (prize/result)?
- ☼ How does dimming myself to avoid peoples' judgments serve me well in the long term?
- ☼ What new mindset would produce the best results for me now?

EXERCISE:
Step 1—Want

Think about what you've been "wanting" for a very long time. Look at your results and connect the two. What is missing?

1. What have I been wanting?

....
....

2. What is my result in this area?

....
....

3. What is missing?

....
....

EXERCISE:
Step 2—Desire

Think about what you desire now or most recently.

1. What do I desire?

....
....

2. What is my result in this area?

....
....

(continued on next page)

> **EXERCISE:**
> ## Step 2—Desire *(continued)*
>
> 3. Am I ecstatic about my results?
>
> If your answer is "no," recall the passionate you, and then consider renewing your commitment.
>
> ....
>
> ....
>
> If your answer is "yes," consider looking at where you'd like some change in your life and commit to that.
>
> ....
>
> ....
>
> 4. What is my renewed commitment?
>
> ....
>
> ....
>
> 5. Where would I like some change in my life?
>
> ....
>
> ....
>
> *(continued on next page)*

While focused on the prize in answering these questions, she changed her attitude about what others think of her. Now, with more confidence in her skills and greatness, she approaches learning with enthusiasm and renewed commitment!

> **EXERCISE:**
> # Step 3—Commit
>
> Think about to what you are and are not committed.
>
> 1. To what am I committed?
>
> ....
> ....
>
> 2. What is my result in this area?
>
> ....
> ....
>
> 3. To what am I not committed?
>
> ....
> ....
>
> 4. What is my result in this area?
>
> ....
> ....

BELIEVE

I'll see it when I believe it.

I imagine myself surrounded by all of life's rewards that have transpired based on "I'll see it when I believe it." I now see the difference between that and "I'll believe it when I see it."

> *faith*—a confident belief in the truth, value, or trustworthiness of a person, an idea or a thing; a belief that does not rest on logical proof or material evidence; a set of principles or beliefs

While working with my clients, I encourage them to take a position of faith. A client of mine came to me with the mindset of "I'll believe it when I see it" in terms of attracting both an agent and a manager for his acting career.

Several months later, he changed his mind and chose to believe *first*. I'm proud to share that he attracted both an agent and a manager!

> ***believe*—to have confidence in the truth or value of something; to expect or suppose; to accept as true or real**

Stepping fully into an idea without proof, and taking actions to realize it, is a proven and successful theory with which I've experimented on several occasions. One August, I booked a one-way ticket to move back to Los Angeles without having a living space secured. Coming from a position of faith, commitment to my idea and belief in myself and my manifestation, several days later I was on the phone with my friend, brainstorming about a place to live. In the midst of our conversation, a light bulb went off when he realized that he had an empty piece of property just waiting for me.

∞

Making a Deal with God

This is one of my favorite stories to share, even though it may seem incongruent with this technique. Listen between the lines.

It was a very snowy winter in Boston and I was living in a two-family house with a very long driveway. Huge, white snowflakes fell for what seemed like weeks. At that time, I was advised not to shovel snow because of my upper back disk disease, yet there I was, shoveling like a torment with no help. I was hurting physically and felt demoralized spiritually because, deep down, I knew there had to be a way out of victim mode and into happiness. There was no way that a good person ought to live like this. *No way!*

In that moment, I placed my shovel down, looked up at the sky and, feeling the wet flakes on my face and with conviction, humor and creativity, I declared out loud, "OK! OK! God, if you are there, if there is actually a God, I am so willing and so committed to believing in you. I am stripped of any solution of peace at this point. So, let's make a deal. If you get me some help shoveling this driveway *right now*, I will believe in you for always. Deal?"

Three seconds later (no kidding), my neighbor, whom I had never met, was standing there at the foot of my driveway with a snow blower.

"Hi. I'm your neighbor, Chris, and I'm here to snow blow your driveway for you."

I laughed so hard and then welcomed him with open arms and a little bit of guilt. I remember how my body became instantly lighter and tingles sizzled through every inch of me. I couldn't believe it! Well, I could and did believe in that moment that I was such a powerful human being, a spirit and a child of God that I actually saw the evidence! By striking a deal, with a dogmatic approach, I got my proof.

THE SECRET OF BELIEVING

Reflecting back on certain occasions when I've declared my desire for something, I now realize that, in those moments, I unconsciously did not believe I could have it . . . thus I did not create it. In believing in myself first rather than waiting for proof, I am manifesting more than I ever imagined.

Still, I have moments when I do not believe, as I look around and dislike what I see in front of me. Yet, I have created all that is in front of me, and that result is derived from what I believed. So, realistically, *I always believe* . . . it just depends on what I am focused. I *believe*.

WANT—DESIRE—COMMIT

In the exercise on page 25 ("The Keys to Freedom, Joy and Bliss" on page 25), I encouraged you to play around with certain words. I am now going to share some ideas on the phrase "want—desire—commit."

> I want something.
> I desire something.
> I eventually commit to something.

want—lack; need

Wanting is the future act of want.

Full of lack and need, I've used this word without realizing that I am in a place of lack and need. Relating to the Law of Attraction (see page 57) ownership and accountability, this word is unsupportive in my visions and goals.

When I habitually think or say I "want," I am most likely in a state of doubt, fear and perhaps laziness. Combining these mindsets, my results manifest over time or sometimes not at all.

desire—long; hunger for; aspire to; request; solicit; seek

Desire has potency and is more often in the "now."

I tend to feel more excited about life when I am full of desire. I'm in a great mood, and have more energy and confidence and a sense of claiming who I am and what is important. This is usually the stepping stone to committing to something.

> ***commit*—to give in trust or charge; to pledge (oneself) to a position on an issue or question**

Commitment is freedom because I am no longer resistant to it.

I'm no longer resistant to commitment because I know I have choice. I know myself well enough to discern what feels "right" and what does not. I know that when I am "on the fence" (*ouch!*), that is exactly where I am: uncertain, uncomfortable and stagnant. *Boring!* I'm giving my power away to the world, waiting for *it* to give *me* something.

SELF-COMPASSION

Compassion is the humane quality of understanding the suffering of others and a strong desire to relieve it. In bringing my personal experience to my coaching, I realize that self-compassion is critical in healing illness, especially depression. I am opening up a very different approach to the issue of depression. In this book, I deal mainly with aspects of the milder or chronic forms of depression. The techniques described here are not considered in any way a replacement for professional treatment for a serious psychological condition. However, my discussed techniques may help avoid the recurrence of depression after coming out of the funk.

When I think I am being compassionate with others, it doesn't necessarily mean that I am being compassionate with myself. Self-compassion is where it all starts; when I have that, I have more compassion for others.

Self-compassion provides focus on my greatness, which, in turn, increases productivity, confidence, joy and creative infusions. It moves me forward, feeling free rather than stalled. I am now ready to be of service. I feel whole when I am of service to myself and others.

The act of self-compassion includes being still with my emotions and stymied thoughts for a sufficient amount of time in order to own them and nix the overload of beating myself up. It is a tender way to own my truth without falling in a 30-foot hole in the ground, feeling like I'll never come out. That, by the way, is my definition of depression.

Here are some examples of mean self-talk turned into compassionate self-talk:

Mean: "No! *No!* You *deserve* this financial rut, you jerk! You messed up your money management again!"
Compassionate: "Calm down. Breathe. I generated twice as much income this year than last year."

Mean: "You can't even stay on track with your exercise for two weeks straight!"
Compassionate: "Hey, I'm human and fall off track. The good news is that I can easily get back on track one step at a time starting today."

Mean: "You shouldn't have gossiped with Alex! *Argghh!* Why? *Why?*"
Compassionate: "I'm asking Alex to support me in keeping my conversations constructive from now on."

Mean: "You don't deserve to be rich or live where you want to or to have a boyfriend. Get your act together, and then maybe, just *maybe*, you'll get what you desire."
Compassionate: "I deserve to have the best life I know possible."

THREE STEPS TOWARD SELF-COMPASSION

Step 1: **Ho'oponopono** (an ancient problem-solving art from the Hawaiian culture, which teaches that life, in fact, can be easy; to make right or to rectify an error by connecting with divinity). Repeat silently over and over: "I'm sorry. Please forgive me (for whatever is going on inside of me that is causing this). I love you. Thank you."

Step 2: **Story * Poof! * Action!** When I am concocting a negative *story* about myself, I instantly *dissolve* it ("You can go now!") and take a simple form of *action* with something I love to do, such as watering my plants, looking at photos or singing a song. This method is ideal to use at the workplace.

Step 3: **Stream-of-consciousness writing** (uninhibited writing with pen or pencil). When I have completed this (usually one to three pages), I then write what I love most about myself and how I positively impact others.

TAKING A GOOD LOOK

When I am harsh with myself, I am usually harsh with others. I project my self-punishment onto them. There is a fine line between self-discipline and self-torture. While I am a fan of self-discipline, honing my skills, refining my approach to life and taking a good look, it does not mean I have to beat myself up along the way. *That* is where I think many people get confused; I know I was. I thought that "taking a good look" meant making myself wrong, punishing myself over and over, swimming in guilt and shame and feeling unworthy of good for forever . . . and a day.

∞

"I'm Doing What I Want to Do!"

Debbie is a very lovely woman and a mother of three kids. I've known Debbie for only two years and have come to appreciate her class, conviction and business smarts. When Debbie was married, she gave all of herself to her family, her friends and her husband, Chris. When the children came along, all of her time was devoted to them. She and her husband became distant, and he had an affair.

Debbie's eyes opened wide. She got her act together and declared, "I'm doing what I want to do!" She embarked upon a part-time job. Being of service in a stimulating environment of adults soon bestowed a feeling of wholeness, greater self-confidence and respect.

She became her own person again and knew confidently that she'd stay strong. One of many realizations was that her husband felt threatened by her betterment and strength; it was no wonder that she stifled herself all those years. Owning up to her "weak link" of acquiescing ways in her marriage, she knew that, if she did not get good with herself, her relationships (especially with her children) were destined to unhappiness.

With compassion, she told Chris, "I'm done. I'm creating a better life for me."

The great news is that Debbie and Chris, childhood sweethearts, had a bond of respect and love for one another. Their divorce was complete within four months with no controlling games, agony, resentment or revenge. They shared love and respect through this trying journey.

Debbie asked her children—seven, nine and 12 years old—questions and was completely open to answering them. There was open communication to express emotions with no secrets; as a family unit, they continued to participate in activities together. Her children are now well adjusted with good grades and vitality for life.

To this day, Debbie and Chris get along very well. He supports her in accomplishing every dream, respects her potential as a woman and is very influential in her entrepreneurial endeavors.

A few years after the divorce, in her first full-time job, Debbie—with her personal approach and business savvy—became #1 in sales and an account executive for another company who soon snagged her away. She is at a time in her life where she has the financial security to pick and choose who, what and where. She has recently founded an all-green cleaning and interior design business with a dear friend of hers.

INTENTION

> "Intent" implies a sustained,
> unbroken commitment or purpose.
>
> "Intention" implies an intermittent resolution
> or an initial aim, a purpose or a plan.

"Intention" is the magic word. Being clear on my intention in every moment for whatever objective or motivation creates an open door between me and what's in front of me—communication, exercise, driving, shopping, speaking, making love, dancing, singing, working, creating, saying "yes" to an invitation, making a request or giving a friend some tough love. Being clear on my intention is necessary when I am playing a big game, and I am in that moment in time when the opportunity arises for a call to my greatness, fully expressing myself in my unique light.

INTENTION—INVENTION

Recall that commitment is freedom and an open gateway toward manifesting a result; declaring my intention sets the stage for invention.

I have wished for something and gotten back something a little different. I have asked someone a question without regard to my intention and have received backlash instead. I have walked into one room from another for something and, once I got in the room, forgot why I was there.

Reflecting back on those occasions, I'll check if I was very clear on my intention; often, I was not. I have heard some inappropriate words in my ears and often ask that person what his/her intention was; they usually don't know. I am courageous enough to ask someone, "What is your intention in saying/

asking/doing that?" I'd say, more often than not, he/she does not know. This question generally provokes the person to stop and think. They often thank me for helping them easily access their intention then and for future reference as well.

Would I buy a new home or vehicle without knowing my intention? Would I choose a new job without a definitive intention? Would I form a new romantic relationship without an obvious intention? How do I know I have the "right" intention?

Well, I ask myself, "What is my intention in buying a new car?" My answer is, "To feel safer and help clean the air." Now, have I covered all bases? Let's check. Does this mean I am going to buy just any car that is safe and in hybrid form? No. Saving money is a great idea! Let's add "economical." What size and color?

Maybe none of these options matter to me at all. Then I am back to the basic intention of buying a new car.

GRATITUDE

Studies show that practicing gratitude on a daily basis plays a big role in improved sleep, enhanced spirituality, connection with others, feelings of love, creating abundance, fewer symptoms of illness, increased alertness and enthusiasm, less depression and stress and a willingness to help others. Gratitude is giving thanks for what is, even if I do not see it.

∞

"A" Student

In August, I began a year-long research study with Katie, a young woman in her last year of a master's program for speech pathology. In considering the value of working with a college student, I thought of Katie since my favorite teaching is on ownership of word and thought.

I was pleased when I learned that Katie's personal commitment is to live her life from a place of gratitude. I encouraged her to write every morning and evening, with feeling, about what and for whom she is grateful, who loves her and whom she loves and how she contributed to society that day.

Her results in responding rather than reacting to those around her are almost effortless now. Furthermore, she feels a greater sense of confidence and has a *significantly* higher grade level than last year (all As!).

∞
"Back Off! I'm Beating Myself Up!"

I've been working with a wonderful comedian and chef named Joe. In 1983, Joe was using cocaine to fulfill what seemed to be missing. Using this outside source for companionship landed him an arrest he would never forget. Joe was hurting and carried this hurt with him into his next two marriages.

In high school and college, Joe was very good at certain things, appearing to be an overall attractive package, yet there was this underlying notion that he *didn't deserve the good*. He remained committed in the pursuit but, when he actually got what he wanted, he didn't maintain the level of commitment because his "I'm not good enough" story was real and thus sabotaged what he just achieved.

He coasted in self-direction with a lack of confidence and resisted working under dictatorship. Two marriages later, and a heartfelt romance that was intended for the future, he backed out under the mindset that the relationship was an obligation rather than an opportunity. He tended to avoid conflict under the pretense that he didn't deserve the good, and thus never asked for what he wanted. As a result, he made decisions in his relationships based on that premise.

Fast-forward to 2003—the pivotal point at his friend's wedding where he saw that his former girlfriend had moved on in her life and with the recent death of his cat. Joe realized that he hadn't been doing anything with his life or for himself. He had been living in the past, dragging it around like dirty laundry and waiting for Opportunity #4 with his former girlfriend, realizing then that it wasn't going to happen. He took a look at how some experiences got him to where he was that day. He realized that he'd be wise to look ahead and create a new life.

Gratitude for his Sicilian heritage and love of cooking sparked an inspiration to create a cookbook of his mother's favorite Sicilian recipes. Emanating from that success, along with his passion for comedy and cooking, he embarked on a deliciously humorous journey.

As the owner and chef of Sicilianaire, he now hosts a multitude of services such as "Girls' Night In," "Cooking from the Cave" (for men) and "Comedy Cooking Classes" at food stores on the west coast and in the St. Louis area. Most recently, someone gifted him the financial sources to bottle and distribute his caponata in the U.S. In the first five weeks, he sold one-third of that amount and the remaining two-thirds was profit. His business has grown quickly by approaching this adventure from his heart.

He now believes that, if he came from a place of entitlement and obligation, he would not have the extraordinary results he has today! Joe told himself the truth, grabbed onto something healthy and loving and created his big game: the "Wide World of Comedy." Now he has purpose and an umbrella in which to thrive in his passion for bringing people together with humor and food, sharing stories and leaving a legend.

∞

Grumpy Curmudgeon or Gracious Champion?
by Jim

A pair of recent events provides me with a great opportunity to write about gratitude. Side by side, these events illustrate what difference gratitude can make, and has made, for me.

My home has been robbed twice over the last several months while I was away at work. Both times, I've come home from work to discover it at the end of a long day. The first time it happened, I was very upset! I lost an expensive video game console I'd recently purchased and a laptop containing all my data—almost a decade of old e-mail, pictures, bookmarks, memories of old girlfriends and a short-lived marriage. At the time, I was already working with a coach. After the break-in, I made a point of exploring the question of how in the heck could I have gratitude for this?

The list is overflowing with ways! I'm grateful for what the robber left. I'm grateful to have given up a lot of the past wrapped up in that computer and have made a clean start on a new one. I'm grateful for the inspiration to get back on my path to finding my dream home—a pursuit I'd been neglecting. I'm grateful for the assistance in reclaiming video game time for better things . . . things more aligned with my purpose and long-term goals.

A few months later, I was robbed again. This time, almost immediately, I was exhilarated. I laughed at the circumstance! I thought the situation was kind of cool—a good story—and I was grateful to have all of that in my life.

Why? Well, for one thing, it was Valentine's Day, and the main thing stolen was my wedding ring from my failed first marriage. I say, "Perfect!" I publish a comic strip, and it was fodder for the strip the next day. I'm grateful for life; it has more laughs than any TV show.

For another thing, after my previous break-in, I'd booby-trapped the house and the burglar fell for it! Suffice to say, the burglar took items that provided clues and left a trail. During the first break-in, the police had nothing to go on. This time was different and I was proud of my accomplishment. I'm grateful for the opportunity to create some safety for my neighbors by luring the robber back to my "honey pot."

I'd also hit a lull in my new-home searching. I'd slacked and, once again, I got the motivation back. I'm grateful for that, too.

Getting robbed the first time felt awful. It took quite a while to work through those feelings. Learning gratitude made all the difference the second time around. My happiness returned so much more quickly. Believing in myself as a capable person has supported me in getting more of what I want. Living gratefully has supported me in wanting (enjoying, appreciating) more of what I get. Life is joy when those two things work together!

P.S. Four months later, I am closing on my first home, and my timing could hardly be better. I found newly completed construction and my gut feeling was unmistakable. This was the place for me. Not only that, I just booked my movers. I will wake up, for the first time ever in this new house, on my birthday. It feels like a storybook, and sticking with my vision worked. I'm so grateful!

SELF-RESPECT

To me, self-respect means a sense of my own dignity, pride, self-esteem or worth. It is treating others the way I'd like to be treated.

To love myself first, and to be good to myself by nurturing my values and what is most important to me, is treating myself with respect. To treat myself with kindness and compassion and staying true to my gifts, uniqueness and inherent rights as a human being is a form of self- respect.

I am treated with respect to the degree I respect me.

∞

Self-respect

In June 2005, I led a workshop in Boston in which I met a lovely woman named Beth. She is a single mother of three girls who is determined to create the best life for them and for herself.

During the workshop, she enthusiastically went to the front of the room and volunteered an example of the phrase, "If I desire a certain change in my life, I must be the change." Beth stated that she'd like her oldest daughter to be respectful toward her and her two sisters.

Now, I had only known Beth for about an hour, but I already determined that she had a low level of self-respect. I gave her some tough love with these words: "If you desire respect from your daughter and others, you must respect yourself first."

That was her moment, her epiphany, and she took the news quite well. She committed to working with me in my coaching program that following November. She declared, "I'm committed to making healthy changes in my life. I'm giving myself six months to financially prepare and we'll start in November."

Beth honored her commitment. I took Beth through a year-long process under the umbrella of "Me with Me." Step by step, she changed her mindset and attitude, developed an ownership word and thought set, created a healthy lifestyle and set goals that were unreasonable but realistic. ("Unreasonable" means going above and beyond one's comfort zone.) She learned and remembered that her experiences come from within. In the past, she looked to men to give her those wonderful felt experiences yet, through our coaching process, staying on track and falling off track, at a certain point she transformed.

She "got" it. Within the year, she bought a home, renovated the basement for her daughter—who was about to have a baby any day—and, through the home-purchase process, she met a wonderful man who values, respects and cherishes her and her daughters as if they're his own.

∞

Beth with Beth
by Beth

When I first saw Janet Caliri's workshop flyer, "What Do You Want More of in Life?" in July 2005, I was ready to begin a new chapter in my life. I just didn't realize it at first.

I remember Janet telling me to ask myself, "What is most important to me right now and am I willing to do what it takes?" The first goal I set for myself was just a stepping stone. I chose to change my financial position and, in doing so, attract positive things into my life. It was time to take the money I made and put it towards creating a life that is rich and fulfilling, leading me and my daughters in the direction that I wanted to go. I only had to believe that right *now* was the time to invest in myself, no matter what the reasons at the time were. I sat down and thought about what is important to me given the place I was at in my life.

My desires at that time were to have better relationships, not only with a significant other, but most importantly with my daughters. I also felt that it was time to buy a home; not just a house, but a place filled with love, both for myself and my daughters.

Since working with Janet, I have achieved so much. Not because I wasn't "able" to in the past, but because I was not focusing on me—being Beth with Beth. I know now that my relationship with others is only as good as my relationship with myself.

I purchased the home that I had always wanted almost two years ago. I found an incredible man to spend the rest of my life with. I've established a wonderful relationship with my oldest daughter and I am actually helping her see how to focus on her needs, understand what makes her happy, and pass that wonderful information on to her son at a very early age.

It was incredible to see that, once my daughter saw me falling in love with myself, she wanted what I had and to share that with those she loves. My relationships with all three of my daughters, my friends, family and coworkers are healthier. I'm communicating more effectively. Life is amazing—I am a wonderful person and truly a gift!

∞

The Best

While growing up in Argentina, Alejandra does not recall *the* moment when she committed to "Ale with Ale." From the age of 20, she was always thinking that her relationships would last if she were smarter, more beautiful, better dressed and the perfect weight and size. "I want to be just like her," she would often think. She continued to look outside of herself for her perfectly exciting experiences of self-worth, but the consistent tape ran inside of her head, saying, "I cannot be *because I am not like them.*"

This all stemmed from the moment when she had a friend over to play, and her mother turned to Ale and said, "Did you notice how graceful Veronica was sitting on the couch? You should copy that." *Should.* Hmmm ... a word that somehow permeates the mind and translates as "I am not good enough, I am never enough and I am obligated to give up my core values and essence so others will approve of me." This permeation develops into disappointment, lack of compassion, resentment, unnecessary pressure, stress and ultimately lack of self-worth, which promotes physical ailments and disease.

One single word can have this profound effect on a human being. Now, let's relate this situation of "you should" taken in the positive context, which ultimately creates an enthusiastic, inspiring leader. That is all well and good *if* the person receiving this message is evolved enough not to take it personally but instead to take it as a gift with positive intention.

Until the age of 21, Ale was always the best honor student, dancer and English speaker. Then, she attended college and realized that there were others who were just as good, if not better, at excelling in certain academic and artistic areas. Slipping into her old ways, she thought, "I can be the best if I have the same pen as she has."

> The natural evolution of life is like laundry—the dirty unwanted parts and the clean desired parts are always necessary.

She went to her father and said, "I'm sorry to disappoint you, Dad."

He replied, "What? Why are you competing with others? Do your best with *you*. That is all you need."

This affirmation was an acceptance of who she was and what she knew deep down inside. Her grades suddenly skyrocketed and she was applauded by three professors at her tribunal final exams.

However, the old story seeped in and she was doing the head dance of mimicking others to feel worthy. After a hurtful break-up with a long-term boyfriend around Valentine's Day, she and two friends were walking down the hall in school and came upon some paper hearts—and one in particular—on the floor.

Her friend picked it up and declared, "This is mine."

The other girl said, "No, it is not. It belongs to Miss Sosa."

Ale replied, "Yes, you are right. My heart was on the floor and now it's here on my heart and always will be!"

Her message that day was, "Always be me!"

Then, in the late 1990s, Ale met a wonderful man at a spiritual camp in which she wore sloppy clothes and no make-up. He thought she was beautiful and they fell in love. Appearing at her door for their first official date, she greeted him wearing make-up.

He was startled and said, "Wow, you're wearing make-up. Why? I like you without make-up."

Alejandra replied, "I know I'm beautiful, but I *like* wearing make-up. It's part of the package. If you don't like it, sorry!"

What eventually led to the end of their romantic relationship was Alejandra's desire for something more substantial than a social security for her image and self-worth. She was now in uncharted territory of not being in a romantic relationship.

"I'm okay. I broke up with him because of love . . . love for myself."

Fast-forward to 2004: her marriage to the love of her life, Matthew. Before declaring their lifelong commitment to each other, she declared, "This is who I am and here is what is important to me."

"Ale with Ale" is constant practice within her marriage as her unconscious fights back once in a while with thoughts like "Maybe I ought to get that coat." Now, she quickly aborts the unhealthy thinking and replaces it with a yoga class in which she laughs at herself, saying, "What the heck was I thinking?"

Two and one-half years ago, before her marriage, Ale shared her "love list" (a list form or paragraph form of who I am being and who my partner is being in the relationship, which usually includes core values such as physical and personality traits, life visions, goals and purpose), which described details about Matthew but nothing about who she was being in that relationship.

I enjoyed hearing it and replied, "That's nice. What kind of partner do *you* intend to be?" A pivotal moment! She declared who she was as a partner and, soon thereafter, attracted her loving husband, Matthew.

The other question she often asks herself when she sees his socks on the floor is, "What would love do right now?"

COMMUNICATION MODEL

A highly effective road to clear and respectful communications.

Intention (purpose, what for)
Data (facts, five senses)
Story (interpretation, perception)
Feeling (emotion)
Suggestion (idea, follow through)

Using the communication model is very effective in having the listener hear me. They are clear on my intention and more open to listening rather than feeling defensive. Here are some opportunities in which I use this model:

- ☼ To create closeness rather than distance between myself and others
- ☼ To create effective change
- ☼ To make a difficult communication with good intention

This model is abridged and modified based on what I learned at the "21st Century Leadership" course, along with what has added the most value to me and my clients. You may search for "communication model" on the Internet and find many descriptions of it.

I'd like to share some examples with you. I'll use basic terms and then a personal experience of my own.

Intention: Hang out with my friend.
Data: The sky is gray and it's raining.
Story: It's a beautiful day.
Feeling: I feel excited.
Suggestion: Let's go to the movies, or maybe do nothing at all.

"Hi, Sue! It's rainy and overcast ... what a beautiful day! I feel excited, so let's do something like go to the movies!"

This may be an odd example as you notice that I think a gray and rainy day is beautiful, while my friend may think it's so awful outside and feels grumpy. Assuming we all have the same perception and feelings ... well, you know what assuming does!

Nonattachment is a way to rid your life of unnecessary unhappiness. As a human being, I get attached to ideas about who I am and what other people should be like. My attachment to those ideas causes most of my day-to-day suffering. It may seem that outer circumstances and reality, and the fact that other people really should be different, are what makes me unhappy; however, it is my ideas about reality that causes the suffering, not the reality itself.

∞

Communication Model and a Lesson in Nonattachment

My friend Laura was feeling sad that she and her friend Michael were becoming distant. She decided that her relationship with him was too important to let go and, with that, she decided to call him with the intention of becoming close again. Here's where the communication model worked very well for the both of them.

"Hi, Michael. I have something to share with the intention to be closer to you. Over the last few months, *I've* called, e-mailed and sent you some letters, but *I* haven't heard back. I honestly think you have no interest in me and my life, and *I* feel really sad and distant from you."

He responded, "Thank you for sharing that, Laura, but I have no interest in being closer to you."

Laura was prepared with a suggestion to start a book club to create a closer relationship; however, sometimes we don't receive a favorable response. The point in having a suggestion or possibility is taking ownership of creating the change.

Notice how she did not say, "*You* haven't called me back. *You* make me feel sad and *you're* the one creating distance between us," or "*You're* just not interested in me!" Instead, she used the words "I" rather than "you."

The wonderful surprise is that she received a 14-page e-mail from Michael two days later, sharing his thoughts on a best-selling book. They have grown closer by the day. Expect the unexpected!

EXERCISE:
Communicate Effectively

Using the communication model, choose a person in your life with whom to practice. Once you have practiced regularly, you'll communicate effortlessly and more effectively.

Intention (purpose, what for)

Data (facts, five senses)

Story (interpretation, perception)

Feeling (emotion)

Suggestion (idea, follow through)

CHAPTER THREE

Ownership

In Chapter Two, you slowly welcomed change with its degree of discomfort. With a few new tools in your pocket for effective communication, self-compassion and daily gratitude, magic of intention and a new attitude about commitment, we'll now ease into the foundation from which I teach: the freedom of ownership and choice.

CLAIM IT!

Ownership is an attitude that feels exactly like freedom, and freedom leads to joy and bliss, which is the very opposite of victim! I desire to be in this state consistently.

Here's an assortment of definitions for ownership: being accountable, taking it on, claiming it, making it mine, possessing it, acknowledging it, admitting it, confessing it, recognizing—often reluctantly—the reality or truth of it and ceasing internal or external opposition.

> Ownership is when I no longer allow gravity to dominate my spirit.

When I own my results, choices, thoughts, words, feelings, emotions and responses, I create an open gateway of flow inside. This conduit is devoid of resistance and obligation, and is full of compassion, gratitude, enthusiasm, motivation, focus and clarity. *Hooray*! Feel it. I feel the vigor of life running through me and out into the world—into my workplace, home, relationships and community.

Here are some examples of opposing questions and statements to myself:
☼ "How do I take ownership in my workplace when my boss is telling me what to do and I think it is the wrong course of action?"

- ☼ "How do I stay alive when my domestic partner threatens to kill me if I leave?"
- ☼ "There's nothing I can do about gas prices. We're all a victim of oil and greed."

Here are some examples of supporting questions and steps I can take:

- ☼ Acknowledge that I do have choice.
- ☼ Nurture my feelings and emotions whether I judge them negatively or positively.
- ☼ Choose who I am being in this moment. Am I reacting like a victim or do I respond and claim it? Own it.
- ☼ The further I expand my line of ownership, the less resistant and more productive and peaceful I become. Do I often or always choose to keep my word? Do I have the mindset that this is *my* company, relationship or country?

Ownership of my thoughts redirects them toward a positive choice, thus healing disease and ailments. Ownership strengthens relationships. Ownership is sexy, powerful and irresistible. Ownership takes courage and faith. Whereas faith is "believing without any evidence," I am relying on uncertainty, which in turn takes courage and thus empowers me and builds my confidence. The ripple effect is increased productivity.

∞

Thoughtful Achiever

A very special woman in my life (my sister Christine) is a blessed wife, mother of three, student, personal trainer and marathon runner. One routine that is very important to her is exercise. When she realized that the reality of having three kids lent itself to less time for her, she decided to wake up each morning before her husband and children, which allows valuable time for Christine to center her thoughts and to exercise.

With this, her productivity and focus increases. She frequently has a balanced life emotionally, physically, spiritually and mentally. This creates a strong model for balance of body, mind and spirit for her children, husband, friends and colleagues. On days that she is feeling off balance, Christine uses prayer as a tool to refocus and keep motivated. What a gift!

∞
An Effective Path to Peace

When giving a talk on ownership and choice for a bank and its customers, I taught them the communication model with the purpose of assisting them in communicating from a place of ownership in and outside of the workplace.

After we went through a demonstration, a woman in the audience shouted out, "Well, things don't just drop on my lap so easily like they do for you!"

I didn't say or imply that this was an easy road; I do know that it's an effective path to peace of mind. Change takes time. Again, it comes back to the discomfort that comes along with change. That being a reality, most people don't change because they would rather feel comfortable.

I responded, "What is most important, and are you willing to feel uncomfortable for some time?"

In the end, she realized that her results were hers and not anyone else's, and that she did have choice in her attitude and reaction to life's never-ending experiences. When I ask myself if I am willing to go through some discomfort, my answer easily comes up "yes" when I am keeping my eye on the prize, the reward.

When I note my age and imagine that I am rewinding a tape of that many years, I am reminded once again that change takes time.

OWNERSHIP IS FREEDOM

Ownership is freedom. When I accept responsibility for *all* of it, I achieve the power to change it (or part of it).

I use certain tools to assist me in assuming an attitude of ownership, including:
- ☼ Forgiving
- ☼ Speaking and thinking in the first person
- ☼ Being aware that I have choice in every moment
- ☼ Laughing at my humanness
- ☼ Having self-compassion
- ☼ Taking time to be quiet and still
- ☼ Frequently asking "What is my intention?" and "What part did I play in this result?"
- ☼ Holding the vision and keeping my commitment
- ☼ Pointing the finger at me (with no blame game)

- ☼ Frequently checking in on red flags
- ☼ Acknowledging my choices
- ☼ Doing whatever it takes to create healthy relationships, both personally and professionally
- ☼ Contributing positively to my community, my country and the planet

Working with an objective and confidential third party, such as a coach, is extremely beneficial in self-realization without feeling guilt or shame. Self-realization is essential to adopting an attitude of ownership, for the more I know myself, the better my life works.

I concede that sometimes I do not want to own my results, choices and behavior, for I associate a negative judgment with it. This is usually when I point the finger at someone or something else, or ignore the situation and think it'll go away. Unfortunately, I know that this only builds upon the issue and it magnifies down the road.

When I claim the aftermath, choices and behavior right away, I have an immediate sense of relief. In that relief, I feel good about my integrity, and freedom is then delivered with a greater sense of compassion from within. I laugh it off easily and continue with my day. Moreover, I easily refrain from beating myself up or steaming and stewing for hours about the situation.

Consequentially, my energy is freed up to tap into my creativity, which is where magic occurs. I naturally step into the zone, engaged in the moment, and here I am living in my potential. In that exhilaration, the experience bubbles up to build upon the creative flow that is already at play, supporting my momentum toward more results.

∞

Waxing the Car

From the age of 3 until 42, David lived his life proving that he was not good enough. Two examples are flunking out of college and never living to his potential in the sports world. Meanwhile, anyone coming in contact with him knew David's brilliance and exceptional talents. Today, David is living a life of accomplishment, contribution, dignity and grace.

Let's rewind a bit. The truth is that some of us blame our parent(s) for our turmoil and self-sabotage. It's usually unconscious and, in David's case, it was. He never once questioned that his results in the "I'm not good enough" mindset had *nothing* to do with his parents.

He would put a new finish on his two cars about twice a year. It would take him eight hours for each car . . . so that's 32 hours of just that. Then he would wash and polish the cars once a week (another two hours per car). What a waste. It would give him an excuse not to get anything done that was important. It was the perfect avoidance system for the procrastinator.

Now let's fast-forward. In 1988, he was turned down three times from his then future wife. She had an opportunity to hang out with him socially and realized he wasn't a jerk after all. They were married in 1993 and, in 2000, she moved to Hollywood to pursue her dream of acting. David never questioned her, his generosity in providing for her and his willingness to slowly dissolve what was important to him in his hometown of Reading, Pennsylvania.

After living a bicoastal life in order to maintain his comedy club and radio syndication, he turned to drugs, drinking and womanizing, thinking "I deserve this." In his entitlement and martyrdom, he gave up all his goodness and light, and put a dark cloud around every part of his life. All of this seemed the easiest route for him . . . again proving that he wasn't good enough. In 2004, his wife requested a divorce and he hit rock bottom.

Immediately, he became "David with David" and stopped drinking, doing drugs, overeating and smoking. He exercised like there was no tomorrow. He became healthy and was consistently delivering amazing radio shows. Thirty days later, he was healthier and sober although still avoiding his truth in his work 18 hours a day.

In March 2004, the light bulb went off and he recorded a three-minute demo of his radio work. He soon received a call from a radio syndication manager in Chicago who had heard of him in high regard. During the conversation, David said to her, "I'm not sure where we're gonna go, but I am very certain you want to go along for this ride!"

In April, he was signed to the biggest sports radio network, Sporting News Radio. His cholesterol levels decreased and he put his life together on his own. In the meantime, his friends were in admiration of his positive changes and results, and encouraged him to attend a transformational seminar to move forward in his potential.

Deep inside, however, David thought he was not doing so well. In May 2004, he decided to stop his nagging friends and attended the weekend transformational seminar, which was life-altering for him. He realized that his mindset of "I'm not good enough" had been his unconscious choice of being and had absolutely nothing to do with his parents.

In committing to "David with David," his juicy pay-off is now living a life full of goodness and light, accomplishment instead of procrastination ("waxing the car"), dignity and grace. He frequently asks himself, "Is this going to give me a life that I love?" If the answer is no, then he makes a choice for his highest good without fear of what others might think or say.

The best part is that he and his former wife are great friends. If David is your friend, is it not true that you'd rather him live a life of integrity, gratitude, contribution and love versus pleasing you in the face of selling his soul? If you prefer him giving up a core value for you, then I suggest reading this book over and over.

Asking myself questions like "Is this going to give me the life that I love?" or "Is this the highest choice for my well being?" are very good tools to utilize for potential, joy and bliss. I recommend these simple questions on a daily basis.

THE MIRACLE OF OWNERSHIP: HOW I OVERCAME DEPRESSION

As a teenager and adult, I had bouts of depression. I was given sleeping pills and antidepressants, and was diagnosed with chronic fatigue syndrome and seasonal affective disorder. Along with this, my body manifested all sorts of physical ailments. Nothing worked. Nothing fixed me.

Ironically, I knew that this seeming hole in my solar plexus was to be filled with love and joy by *me*, yet I didn't have a clue how to do that. I was a citizen in a society that primarily looks to the outside rather than the inside to "fix" problems.

At the age of 35, I participated in a leadership and personal development seminar, in which I experienced myself in my lightness and darkness for seven days. Though I was uncomfortable throughout most of this program, much to my surprise, I began to feel a sense of control and a deeper love for myself. This further supports my proven theory that the more I know myself, the better my life works.

Here are some of the tools I gathered and apply in my life:

I have choice in every moment—choice about my feelings and thoughts, thus choice about what to do with them. I used to think that people made me feel or think a certain way, but that was when I lived life in the role of a victim. Now, *no one makes me feel a certain way*. When I operate in life as a victim, I am giving my power away and feeling weak, unproductive and unconfident.

I am waiting for someone or something to make me feel a certain way or to make something happen for me. There is so much resistance in this . . . the very opposite of freedom.

I may ask myself, "Do I want to heal and become healthy, whole and sound?" What if the answer is "no"?

I realize that, at some point in my life, I did not want to be healthy and whole because that meant I had more responsibility for my greatness. I would think:

- ☼ "People have extremely high expectations of me; I've got to keep them low."
- ☼ "I am highly sensitive to other people's emotions; I've got to stay in martyrdom, taking it all on instead of just my own."
- ☼ "People are shunning me; I feel safe by not expressing myself."

I believe that we are all here to contribute. Each and every one of us has a unique gift that lends itself to strengthening the fabric of goodwill.

Another tool I use is being conscious of my core essence. The first step was to discover who I am at my core (my mojo) and, as I began to feel alive and fulfilled, this vehicle continues to carry me through my mission. What follows is bliss as a consequence of and in proportion to my connection with purpose.

The moment I committed to ownership—to owning my life—is the moment the depression melted away. I haven't had a bout of depression since. I did not need medication to take away my pain. I took away my daily pain and depression through applying ownership tools and concepts in my life.

CHOICE

> *choice*—an act or instance of choosing; the right, power, or opportunity to choose; alternative; option; preference

The day I realized I had choice in every moment, I felt a weight that subsided in minutes, like a baby bird flying from the nest for the first time. I always have choice. I may not like my choices and essentially may pay a high price for my choices, but I do have choice. My choices are made either consciously or unconsciously but, the more I listen to my inner voice, the sounder choices I make.

> **EXERCISE:**
>
> # I Have Choice in Every Moment
>
> Choose to choose, then choose again (or not). When you are not choosing, you are still choosing something.
>
> 1. What do I have choice about?
>
> ....
>
> ....
>
> 2. What choices have I made that I respect?
>
> ....
>
> ....
>
> 3. What choices have I made that I am not happy about?
>
> ....

∞

One Simple Choice
by Alisha

As a 28-year-old single mother, and just barely having my divorce finalized from a long, dragged out battle of three years, I realized that it is all a choice . . . all of it . . . all decisions that are made in life. One simple choice.

The choice is to choose my own freedom of peace, who enters it and who is not welcome. My situation was up and down. I was so unstable to anyone entering my space. I could not have gone further from my values. Born in Utah and being raised Mormon, I had a lot of guilt and shame. During the three-year divorce battle, my patterns became worse than my alcoholic ex-husband, who is now sober and doing wonderfully. I had patterns of man after man after man. I used them while hiding my own dark secrets of unhappiness.

Fast-forward to six months later: I discovered a man who was all *love*. All he had to give me was love. Love that I felt when I was 18! Love has many meanings, as you and I know, but what does it mean to you? Once you understand that meaning, will you follow through with your own creation of it, or will you allow your old patterns to destroy what once was so beautiful and created on your own?

My choice, after feeling like I have had time to heal, was to expand myself and my love. The excitement of expanding my career and my love all at the same time was so liberating that I became clear! *So I thought.* This choice came with sacrifice and suffering. I moved to California and chose to leave my son behind temporarily with his father, the man whom I fought three years for my son's custody. This never felt natural to my spirit, but I choose to flow with life. I choose to maintain the peace. I swore I would never allow my spirit to break again. I was going to be OK! Freedom to choose! Well, so I thought . . .

I had to experience this to understand that freedom of the mind is achievable along with learning what made me whole as a person. The choice I made three months *after* living in California and trying to relocate my son was causing my child stress through comments like, "Mommy, I want to live in California and Daddy won't let me." He is three years old. Should he be worrying? I found myself in another custody battle (this time in front of a judge) and painfully learning lessons again. The man I love and my beautiful child are most important in my life; however, remembering to love my spirit allows me to make clear choices when faced with the realization of the situation.

My lesson to be learned was, "There is no separation." Utah and California, custody of my son and being with my soul mate, loving what is and the choices I make. I chose to move back to Utah and am currently "loving what is" along with my soul mate who resides in California. These choices are all connected through our love and our spirit. That is my choice. That is my simple truth.

I will teach this lesson to my son because I have learned through difficult decisions and choices that we have the skill to choose what is connected and what is not.

∞

To the Rescue!

by Ortalia

I have been a dysfunctional codependent all of my life, rescuing loved ones, left and right. Feeling in control, and all knowing. I believed I was such a "good Samaritan." In the process, I completely neglected *me*! I was absent to my life, to my loved ones.

Recently, I have had some powerful and painful realizations. In seeing others as weak, helpless victims who needed me in order to survive (how egotistical!), I was mirroring back that I was a weak, helpless victim . . . as I recognized them to be. I chose to have difficult, painful and liberating communications with each one whom I have held in that view.

I still feel the chills of spirit through me right now as I am writing this. Being accountable for my actions, taking my power back and *returning their power reins to them* has taken me to a level that I have not been in this incarnation.

I realize now in every fiber of my being that *I am as good to others as I am to myself!*

Immediately following our conversations, I have seen such transformation in them. Wow! Our relationships evolved to another level of love and respect. Gone is the resentful, caged feeling I have had all my adult life . . . *all my life.*

I am feeling the juices of creativity surging in my veins. I feel excited and I am in the process of writing my next book, which, once complete, will serve me and so many others. I am feeling like a clear channel to bring forth this next amazing body of work.

I feel excited and so thankful. I have forgiven myself, and I am celebrating my big win . . .

LAW OF ATTRACTION

By definition, "Law of Attraction" means "like attracts like," "I make real that to which I put my attention" or "What I focus on, I get." I see its similarity to ownership

> The way to gratification is through gratitude.

("I attract to me that which occurs and own all of those results"). This law is not exclusively about the power of positive thinking. The only way to gain evidence is to experiment with it. At first, it is most likely a trial-and-error period, but soon I see the evidence. This law is primarily a *function*. You may want to review "Want—Desire—Commit" in Chapter Two (page 33).

Through my own experimentation, I have concluded that the magic is in the "dreamy" versus "alert" state. Another way of saying that is "unintentional" versus "intentional." Living in my awareness and greatness is an existence. I used to believe that the alert thought-feeling-action is the fastest way to materialize. I have studied the difference in results and found that the dreamy thought-feeling materializes more frequently and rapidly than the alert.

Why? As a human, sometimes I doubt or worry when I am fixated on something I want. I'm usually in a state of lack or need. (In the dreamy state, there is no fixation, thus no doubt or worry.) Furthermore, direct action is not possible in the dreamy state as I am clearly not aware enough to take action toward that.

With that said, when I intentionally focus upon a positive desired result, there is most likely resistance, doubt or attachment to it. If that is the case, I end up attracting what I don't like or staying neutral. With the unintentional thought and feeling, there is *zero* resistance or attachment. This surrendered, joyous state provides an open gateway for the positive outcome to appear while I am simply doing my thing and enjoying life.

Here is another example: A friend of mine had been unintentionally envisioning more plants in her home with a feeling of joy and relaxation. A couple of weeks later, she got a call from a friend who offered all of his plants to her as he was preparing to move from his home. She realized then that she was unconsciously using the Law of Attraction!

One of my clients, a security systems software developer at a world-renowned company, was recently relocated to a different office to utilize the full potential of his unique skills. He was chosen to develop the world's first thread-modeling exercise for new software. I asked him what he thought led up to these results and he shared that, in his "sleepy" state, he had consistent feelings of curiosity and thoughts of making a difference in the world. There was no initial, direct action taken on his part, yet it all fell into place.

How does intuition play a role in the Law of Attraction? My intuition or gut feeling is emotional guidance for me. Thought and feeling are already at play, and all that is left to do is take action, which may be inaction.

An example: I had been admiring rings for sale at a local café gift shop. For months I searched for the perfect shape, color, size and price. One day, I felt moved to walk there when a little voice said, "Wear your Inside Out Community Arts t-shirt." This was a quick and random message that I was ready to dismiss. I acquiesced and put on that t-shirt. I found my perfect ring and it turns out the woman behind the counter is an old friend of the cofounder of Inside Out. As a reward for the work I do with the youth, she gave me a 20% discount!

We'll expand on intuition in Chapter Five on page 78.

∞
Entitled Daughter

"Like attracts like" must be used with gratitude in order for it to take the form I'd like. I have a client, Michelle, who puts out a great deal of love and care toward her family. She claims she doesn't get it back. She feels that she deserves it because they are her family, and they should love and care for her just as much as she does for them, especially because she gives it.

"I give and give and give to my family. They don't give back and I don't feel appreciated." I asked Michelle why she would give her power away to them by waiting to feel appreciated. I suggested that she may want to give to others because she likes to, not because she is obligated. Expecting something directly back from that source is being closed off to receiving.

So why isn't the Law of Attraction working for her? She is coming from a place of entitlement, which is opposite of gratitude. When I think I am entitled to something, I become frustrated with an expectation on return; thus, I am not grateful. Therefore, the universe is giving back that exact experience of frustration. Furthermore, I do not always receive back from the source to which I give.

Michelle is certainly receiving love and care from a different source. Therefore, I suggested being open to how things show up. Like most people, I may not be aware when I have an entitled attitude, so checking in on my level of gratitude is a great yardstick.

MANIFESTATION

I manifest not by attempting to attract *to* me but by expressing *out* from me. Consequentially, manifesting is complete only when there is a change in consciousness.

∞
Unintentional Envisioning

One of my "dreams" was to meet Neale Donald Walsh, the author of *Conversations with God*, a life-altering book I read in 1997. My only desire was to give him a big hug and a "thank you." Last October, this book was being released as a movie, with a special screening at Agape International Spiritual Center in

> Be open to how things show up!

Los Angeles. I organized a bunch of friends to go with me, and never once imagined or envisioned all of us sitting in the center watching this movie together.

When we were all standing in line, we were told that the seats were sold out and I didn't see the movie. Before my eyes, Neale Donald Walsh came out to greet us in the parking lot, answering questions and autographing books. I had the opportunity to genuinely thank him for his positive impact on my life. I then realized that what I had been unintentionally envisioning was meeting Neale Donald Walsh!

∞

Authority Issues
Anonymous

I attracted being unemployed through focusing on what I did not want. While searching for a new career in mutual funds wholesaling, my resistance to authority, along with thinking men who had a lot to prove to me, was unconsciously in my way of getting just that.

After complaining and thinking for a while that life was unfair, I saw my unemployment as an opportunity to clean my slate. First, I made a list of desires, such as a position where I was independent, self-expressed, making a difference in the world, constructively actualizing control, recognition and achievement and generating a six-figure income. I put that out to the universe and, in less than a month, I was hired by a company that is a leader in socially responsible investments.

Rewind. When the opportunity arose to apply for this job, I was reluctant because they did not have a wholesaler position, and I thought that working for a small company with bigger territory would not suit my needs. Then, the light bulb went off. This actually presented more than what I asked for. All the while, my resistance to authority and competitive nature with men came up regularly but, this time around, I embraced it and became present to my intention and approached my work from that place. In the first year, I became the top producer, overseeing 45% of the country's mutual fund assets; within three years, I was the first female to attend the annual corporate conference representing this company.

INTEGRITY

The dictionary's definition of "integrity" is completeness, congruence, absoluteness, totality, honor, uprightness, honesty, purity and virtue. I define integrity as "walking my talk," "having my actions speak louder than words" and "honoring my commitments and word."

Integrity is the foremost catalyst to trust and respect. Recall the people in your life whom you respect and trust the most. Do they possess integrity? Most likely, the answer is "yes." Integrity is a value that I hold highly; sometimes I am blind to discerning my relationship with others.

For example, if I am developing a new personal relationship with "Mary," and she is frequently breaking plans and not doing what she says she would, perhaps I am the type of person who would continue to give Mary the benefit of the doubt and ignore the red flags. Perhaps I am a person who has a boundary in which I'll let it go a few times, then realize that this person really doesn't mean what they say and bid them well. Perhaps I am a person who is an integrity control freak and who doesn't give an inch to Mary, and writes her off immediately after one incident.

I give more leeway to those with whom I've been in a congruent relationship because I've already built the trust and respect. When I am forming a new relationship, I observe and then believe their walk rather than their talk. I trust my gut and my intuition. My intuition is my friend. It is within me for a reason . . . not just something that stuck onto me like Velcro. I am born with intuition to use when I have or don't have data (the five senses of smelling, touching, tasting, seeing and hearing).

Actions speak louder than words. I know, from personal experience, that this is true; therefore, I allow less flexibility for those with whom I am creating a new relationship. This is a compassionate balance between being a control freak and an idealist ignoring the red flags. I prefer someone who is confident and helpful and who balances these qualities with humility and grace.

As an idealist, I believe in people's potential the way dogs believe in their masters. I was strongly encouraged to tell myself the truth about the people coming into my life and about those who are already there. I can love them until the cows come home. I can believe in them as much as I know my name and date of birth. *What does my gut say?*

I was consistently out of integrity for many years but did not know it. I was unconscious. (I did not know myself well.) People still loved me and believed in me, yet some were not willing to tolerate feeling disrespected or they lost their trust in me. That is okay. I understand their choices better now than I did back then, when I felt abandoned and undervalued.

I see now that they made wise choices, which actually supported me in growing into my potential by seeing that I was not walking my talk. I was not being who I believed I was. I in turn have let go of a few clients based on the value of integrity. Coaching is results-based and forward-moving, depending on the level of investment of the client. Results speak, and results are not created while hiding behind closed doors. It would not serve them well if I were to support their scarce participation in the coaching program. Besides, I can only serve one who is open to being served.

> Commitment is freedom because I am no longer in resistance to it.

BEING BIGGER THAN MY REASONS

Intentions are a good friend for making wise choices. Reasons can be ghastly when used to justify not living in my essence or not taking ownership of a situation.

Reasons are not the same as intention or purpose.

I grew up with reasons all around me, and I certainly had my fair share of being about them. It's like a domino effect: I am about my reasons and then so are you. I get to be right about my reasons and not take notice of how I'm impeding what is most important to me. My relationships soon enable staying small.

Now, I am mindful in those moments where I want to be about my reasons:
- Is it my intuition?
- Am I afraid?
- Am I avoiding?
- Am I tired?
- Am I too busy to take a break and be social?
- Is it the default of "I should" or "What if?"
- Am I living in the "why" and never moving forward until I get the answer to the reason why?

When I live in my "why," I am floating in the "why" pool and swimming up a "why" stream, arising to the stagnation of life. I get to be safe and unaccountable, remain unmotivated, and wonder why my life is not working in the way I want it. Then I give more reasons for that. When a child asks

"Why?" that child is looking to understand the parent's choice within that request or command. When the parent consistently gives the child reasons, the child gets used to justifying his own behavior, thus living in the "why" instead of accepting what is or discovering the answer on his own. A successful technique is to ask a question followed by a compliment or encouragement. For example, "You're a smart kid. What do you think?"

On a slightly different angle, there's the *automated* reason used when answering a question or receiving a comment. For example:

Joe: "Did you read my newsletter?"

Kathy: "No. I've got hundreds of e-mails to read and I've been working a lot this last week."

If Kathy were being bigger than her reasons, her answer would look like, "No, no yet," and then leave it at that. She assumed the position of being apologetic when Joe was simply asking her a question and most likely was looking to engage in conversation.

I work with a lovely young actor who has developed her awareness in the "reasons" department. As a result, one late evening, her friend invited her to go out to a particular bar to see some friends. My client at first was all about the reasons not to go (she was tired; it was late; she didn't have make-up on).

As her friend said, "C'mon, just one hour and then we'll leave," she remembered that she had options and that this was an opportunity to meet new people. She was actually approached by a guy who claimed he was a producer who was starting to film a feature that next month, and that she'd be great for the supporting role. My client, based on her past experiences, rudely shrugged it off as just another pick-up line, again being about her reasons. She then stepped into being bigger than her reasons, said "yes" to auditioning, and booked the job as the supporting actor!

∞

I Should

My client, Sherry, was promoted to director in her company. During this time, she had gone from living in peace and balance to having regular low energy and being in her head negatively.

I asked her if her promotion was truly what she wanted, and she said "yes." I encouraged her to shift her thinking and speaking, eliminating words that imply inability and resistance. As our coaching program developed, I

> **EXERCISE:**
> # Keeping My Word with Ease (Step 1)
>
> In Chapter Six (page 108), we'll delve deeper into this exercise by using a new technique. For now, a "joyful experience" is a juicy feeling (for example, connection, intensity or accomplishment). Ask yourself the following questions:
>
> 1. When was a time that I broke my word/commitment?
>
> ....
>
> ....
>
> 2. What was my reason?
>
> ....
>
> ....
>
> 3. Is it true that I made my reason more important than keeping my word?
>
> ....
>
> ....
>
> *(continued on next page)*

noticed that she shared her reasons for not doing this or that while complaining of fatigue and frustration.

I concluded that her fatigue was a result of negative thinking, a sense of obligation and constant attempts to gain recognition through sharing her reasons of not keeping her word or commitment to herself. She was hanging on to this unconscious reason to gain recognition destructively. She was keeping her word to others but not to herself. No wonder she was tired!

> **EXERCISE:**
>
> ## Keeping My Word with Ease (Step 1) *(continued)*
>
> 4. What do I think would happen if I made my word more important than my reason?
>
> ....
>
> ....
>
> 5. How would I feel?
>
> ....
>
> ....
>
> 6. Of what joyful experience(s) would I be conscious to motivate myself to keep my word and be bigger than my reasons?
>
> ....
>
> ....
>
> 7. When *was* I in touch with a joyful experience(s) such that I kept my word and was bigger than my reasons?
>
> ....
>
> ....

I encouraged her to apply all the tools I was giving her—no matter how tired she was, how busy she was or if her kids were sick—by being bigger than her reasons. Committing to this process would ultimately yield the positive results she so desired. Through full participation and patience, she would realize and prove, once and for all, that she could have her reality life (even if life intruded) *and* live with peace of mind and balance.

She gave up her need for recognition (in an unhealthy way) and stepped down in her title at the workplace, allowing more time to do what she loves to do. To this day, she shares her happiness in choosing joy and peace of mind.

CHAPTER FOUR

The Gift of Thoughts and Words

Chapter Three was chock full of methods and true experiences to reveal that ownership, choice, integrity, commitment and being unreasonable are the *attitudes* to freedom. The Law of Attraction is primarily a *function,* and manifestation is whole only when there is a *change in consciousness*.

This chapter expands on the benefits of consciousness, using the Law of Attraction, the necessity of ego and the proof that you have the power to change your thoughts and words in order to create a different result.

NEW THOUGHT LEADS TO NEW RESULTS

I recognize that habits are a natural conditioning from generation to generation. This, of course, is why experts say it usually takes at least 21 days with consistent repetition to make or break a habit. I support this successful theory in my "21 Days to Yes!" program (See "Appendix A" on page 124.).

Habits are naturally formed from unconscious thoughts starting from childhood—thoughts and habits embedded in our subconscious mind. What I focus on, I get. When I focus on gratitude and use words like "thank you," I get more of what I desire. When I focus on words like "I don't have," then I get just that . . . *nothing*. I see thoughts and words as a gift, not only to communicate through speaking or writing, but as a method to create what I'd like to make manifest.

THE GIFT OF THOUGHTS AND WORDS

WHAT I FOCUS ON, I GET

Thoughts are the most potent form of energy. Every thought casts a message to the universal quantum field. Applying the Law of Attraction here, we are now attracting a form of our thought. Since "what I focus on, I get," I attract both positive and negative results—whether they appear as an emotional state or a physical form. When I bring passionate feeling to my thoughts, the results are accelerated. When I take action with the thought and feeling combined, my results materialize more rapidly.

Applying the attitude of ownership, I am now consciously making choices and owning those with the words I speak. An example is, "I can't come into work today because I am sick." Think about this in the context of living a life of freedom. Is it true that I *cannot* go into work, or is it true that I am *choosing* to stay home and take care of myself?

I often hear those voice mail messages that say, "I am unable to come to the phone right now." Think methodically about this statement. Is it true that this person is actually *unable* to come to the phone, or is it true that this person is just simply *unavailable* or *unwilling* to take the call right now?

When I begin to use words that truly reflect my choices, I build self-respect and gain it from others. I also become more conscious of having choice, which alleviates the conditioned attitude of obligation and thus develops courage.

∞

Prisoner of Unhealthy Thoughts

For what seemed like an eternity, I was playing the role of victim with my health issues. I had degenerative disk disease in my thoracic spine and, on a daily basis, lived as if I were extremely limited. At that time, I was working in radiology in which I was required to wear a heavy, lead apron for eight hours a day. I felt resentful toward my job, my circumstance and those whom I thought did not understand my pain. I thought, "Poor me." I thought I couldn't drive for longer than an hour, or travel on a plane for an extended period of time, because my back hurt so much from sitting up. I thought I could not exercise or sleep in a bed other than mine.

All of this was a result of my thoughts and what I was voicing out loud. I was allowing my back to run me rather than run it! Concurrently, I was diag-

> **EXERCISE:**
> # Experimenting with Words
>
> Take notice of your thought patterns for one day. Play with this experiment (as encouraged in "The Keys to Freedom, Joy and Bliss" on page 25), have fun and take note of what happens! You may wish to choose one word or tool per day or per week, and then change it for something new when you have internalized your first experiment.
>
> Be patient; reprogramming your mind takes time. You will soon notice that you feel differently and are attracting more of what you like and less of what no longer works for you!

nosed with seasonal affective disorder, Epstein-Barr virus, probable lupus and chronic fatigue syndrome. I had it all.

One day, I went for a regular visit to my orthopedic surgeon, who decided to give me sleeping pills as I was having trouble sleeping. (The truth is that I had sleeping issues since childhood.) Off I went to the pharmacy and got my prescription filled. As I was walking out the door, I saw a trash can and, in that moment, took ownership for my health. I threw the bottle in the can and smiled with exhilaration as I exited.

This was the flip of the switch—the exact moment I claimed my life! I felt so powerful in that moment because I was running my body . . . it wasn't running me anymore!

I visited a sleep specialist and listed all the sleep problems I had since I was three years old: insomnia, nightmares, sleep walking and talking in my sleep. He put me on a 21-day strict schedule in which I was to wake up at the same time every day and go to sleep at the same time every night, regardless of my work and social life. He said "There are only three things allowed in bed: sleeping, being sick and making love."

> Long ago in a galaxy far away, a great Jedi master said, "Do or do not. There is no try."

After two weeks, I went to bed any time I wanted, but I was to wake up at the same time. This system worked! My boyfriend at the time encouraged me to go to bed in a "thinking" position and allow myself to think and spin my brain for as long as necessary. Once I was done, I was to change my body position in order for my brain to recognize sleeping time versus thinking time. Another brilliant strategy!

All of my sleeping "problems" were healed through my commitment of well-being without medication or anything outside of me.

SAY "I"

In January 2007, I completed training to be an artist leader at Inside Out Community Arts. Through free visual performance arts workshops, Inside Out is dedicated to provide youths from all backgrounds the tools, confidence and inspiration to make a positive difference in their communities and the world . . . from the inside out.

One workshop entitled "Nature" is focused on bringing the experience of "me to me," using nature as the vehicle. Like a monologue, the youths own and share their experiences in the first person rather than using the second or third person. This appears to be the workshop in which the students have their first emotional breakthrough and reveal their truth.

This is no surprise. As a society, on the whole, I am conditioned to speak in the second or third person as I am told that it is selfish or arrogant to speak in the first person. Over time, I have been conditioned to look outside of myself and, once I look in, I may not like what I see. Even if it is positive, I think I am not allowed to acknowledge my greatness. As a result, I continue to speak and think in the "you," "they" and "we" . . . unconsciously avoiding my truth.

If I were to make the change in my thoughts and words, even just one switch from the third to the first person, the fabric of goodwill would strengthen. Think about it! Every time I think or say "I," I claim my experience. Regardless of it being negative or positive, there is a genesis for freedom and peace of mind.

Now imagine my mind, body and spirit filled with a sense of freedom. "I am standing in the snow, breathing in the cold air and smelling the wood-burning fire. No one is around and I am alone for miles." Now the opposite experience: "You're standing in the snow, breathing in the cold air and no one is around for miles. You smell the wood-burning stove and wonder when someone will come rescue you."

Feel the difference? Notice I did not ask, "Hear the difference?" It's not about what I hear; it's about what I feel. I feel differently when I own my thoughts and results.

YOU MAKE ME

Imagine every musician writing their lyrics from a place of ownership. Think about it. Music is highly influential in this world. People listen to it for various reasons, ranging from creative expression, relaxation and calming the mind to making love, dancing, inspiring others and connecting. Knowing that almost every person on this planet listens to music, which reaches the subconscious mind and provokes memory, what would happen if the lyrics were in the first person and free of externalizations like "You make me," "I can't," "He did me wrong," "I'm not able to see you again," "Don't leave me" or "She makes me feel so good"?

I admit that perhaps the music may have a totally different flavor, yet the message would be superior in delivery. Add the flavor of ownership, swirling inside the chorus and verses, feeling the beat of humanity and vulnerability, and I would still easily relate to what the music folks are talking about. Music has a way of validating my humanness.

What would humanity on this planet be like if only this one change occurred? I know the potential. I have the urge to call up Jewel and Bono and share this amazing potential for goodwill. That would well suit my purpose of igniting human potential!

Consider the words in the song, "(You Make Me Feel Like) A Natural Woman" (lyrics by Carole King). For every immature female listening to this song, there is a possibility that she thinks the only way to feel "natural" is through a relationship with this particular man. Does that serve her highest good? If she were enlightened enough to know that it is simply a passionate statement about how she feels, no harm is done. However, if, throughout the years, she fantasized about a man making her feel "natural," and never realized that the experience of feeling "natural" comes from within, she may continue to look outside of herself for that experience. Most likely, she has gone through a myriad of relationships, ending in disappointment for how she was feeling with that man, thinking it was *him* not giving *her* something. Sound familiar?

Another example is the Willie Dixon song, "I Can't Quit You Baby." Let's analyze the original lyrics and then offer examples of how to turn them into "ownership" lyrics:

- ☼ *Original lyric:* "I can't quit you baby."
  Ownership lyric: "There's no way to quit you baby."

Ownership lyric: "I don't know how to quit you baby."
Ownership lyric: "It's easy to quit you baby."

☼ *Original lyric:* "I said you messed up my happy home."
Ownership lyric: "My happy home is messed up."

☼ *Original lyric:* "You made me mistreat my only child."
Ownership lyric: "I mistreated my only child."

☼ *Original lyric:* "You built my hopes so high."
Ownership lyric: "I built my hopes so high."

☼ *Original lyric:* "Baby, then you let me down so low."
Ownership lyric: "I feel so defeated."

I AM

There is a great chance of getting what I desire when I begin to think and speak in "I."

"I am" are the most powerful, creative words in the universe. Any time I think or speak "I am," I am in the process of manifesting that thought, be it negative or positive. If I think "I am tired," then I am creating an experience of tiredness. If I think "I am wonderful!," then I am creating an experience of joy.

My negative judgments keep me from joy.

The beauty of "I am" is its power of present-tense thought. I realize that the more I think and speak in the present tense, the quicker I create results. When I am thinking "I will," I am looking into the future without commitment. Surely, I may commit to something, such as a goal, and plan it for the future; however, it is more likely to manifest when I speak in the present tense about it.

Which is more powerful? "I will finish my book next year" or "I am completing my book on February 15th"? How about "Someday, I will go parasailing" or "I am parasailing in January"?

Choose a date! Make *time*lines (not *dead*lines). Timelines harness my commitment and fuel me forward. Without them, I am less likely to move forward in the journey and remain in check with my purpose. However, it is not essential to hold onto reaching each goal or task within the timeline.

EXERCISE:
Flip Side

Listed below are some examples of "victim" versus "ownership" statements. The second line in each example (*Ownership*) is a mindset to create desired results and trust. Trust between people is formed by taking ownership for choices. Desired results are produced when I embrace taking responsibility for my words.

In the following examples, experiment with the ownership ("flip side") of each victim statement. I suggest choosing one or two and using their context in your daily life for one week. Be sure to journal and note your results (e.g., emotions, general attitude, shift in relationships and job).

Example #1:
Victim: "I want to be able to go make some money off of my book, but I can't because of . . ."
Ownership: "I am committed to generating income from my book."

Example #2:
Victim: "I am not able to go to the party,"
Ownership: "I am not available to go to the party."

Example #3:
Victim: "I just can't work and do laundry and feed the kids all at once and expect to be pleasant for my husband."
Ownership: "I'm not willing to scramble and give up my alone time."

(continued on next page)

THE GIFT OF THOUGHTS AND WORDS

EXERCISE:
Flip Side *(continued)*

Example #4:
Victim: "I should go to bed now."
Ownership: "I think it's a good idea to go to bed now."

Example #5:
Victim: "I didn't write it in my calendar because I didn't have it with me at the time of our call and then I had to rush out to pick up my son."
Ownership: "I didn't write it in my calendar."

Example #6:
Victim: "I'll feel obligated if I do that, so I should not get too involved.""
Ownership: "What works really well for me is talking about boundaries right up front."

Example #7:
Victim: "Talking to a room full of people makes me feel intimidated."
Ownership: "I feel intimidated talking to a room full of people."

Example #8:
Victim: "I can't tell her how I really feel because she isn't able to handle it."
Ownership: "If I tell her how I really feel, she may get upset."

CHAPTER FIVE

Raising My Consciousness

In Chapter Four, I imagine it became evident that you have choice to either claim your life or live like a victim. Which do you choose? Are you willing to be a little uncomfortable reprogramming, experimenting and proving your potential to yourself by seeing the tangible results? It's easier to make choices and change when *you know yourself well*. That includes the traits you dislike and usually avoid. Those traits are just as useful as those you do like!

KNOW THYSELF

The more I know myself, the better my life works. The more information I have about myself, the more I have to work with. To understand myself is to understand others. Furthermore, I am less likely to take things personally. For example, when I know my values, habits, boundaries, purpose, blind spots, liabilities and strengths, I am better positioned to handle such things as communication styles in relationships and personalities at the workplace.

One thing I know about myself, which is not often conscious but often brought to my attention, is when I think I am *feeling* sensitive and vulnerable, I am often protecting myself by *being* aggressive and, in my communication, tend to push people away. Since I know this about myself, I am wise to immediately vocalize that I am feeling sensitive and would like some support.

SIXTH SENSE

Carl Jung, the founder of analytical psychology, proposed that there are four main functions of consciousness:

Perceiving functions: (1) sensation and (2) intuition

Judging functions: (3) thinking and (4) feeling

All of the functions are interwoven in my abridged communication model (except the absence of (2) intuition):

(1) "Sensation" is the five traditional senses (seeing, hearing, smelling, touching and tasting)

(3) "Thinking" is my story or interpretation.

(4) "Feeling" is emotion.

Intention (purpose, what for)
Data (facts, five senses)
Story (interpretation, perception)
Feeling (emotion)
Suggestion (idea, follow through)

I'd like to concentrate on intuition within the context of consciousness and effective communication. As noted, intuition has no definitive data; therefore, the "data/story/feeling" component of this model is null and void, and is replaced with "intuition" (such as gut feeling, inner voice and hunch).

If I plug "intuition" (a knowing immediately without reasoning) into those three slots, here's what happens:

Intention: "To update you on where I'm at with our plans."

Intuition: "I have a very strong gut instinct not to drive tonight."

Suggestion: "I stay at home alone or you come over here."

Trusting my perceiving functions can feel risky at times because I have no facts to back me up in my communication. Taking a stand and making a choice, based on my sensation and intuition only, strengthens my level of ownership. With intuition, I get to be right!

∞

Trusting My Gut

This year, I was training and raising money for Inside Out Community Arts by way of cycling in the Los Angeles Marathon. I put forth the fundraising letter to many people and trained regularly. A week before the marathon, I was still hesitant to tune up my bike, which was out of character for me not to be all prepared. Right in the middle of a coaching call, I remembered this prominent message: "Do *not* bike the Los Angeles marathon!" This message

EXERCISE:
Preparatory Questions

It's a good idea to know what you desire and to what you are committed, so ask yourself the following questions. Answer each question with your *first immediate thought* and then add other insights later. There is no right/wrong, good/bad answer, only your truth. This exercise takes less than 15 minutes.

1. What do I desire more of in my life?

   ....

   ....

2. What change do I intend to create?

   ....

   ....

3. Which area of my life works the least well?

   ....

   ....

4. What does my life purpose look like to me? (This is an experience that has a great sense of meaning and contribution.)

   ....

   ....

5. What action steps do I have in place to support my life purpose?

   ....

   ....

(continued on next page)

EXERCISE:
Preparatory Questions *(continued)*

6. What results do I want through reading this book?

   ....

   ....

7. What is my goal for one year? (This is not a wish or a hope. Think *big*.)

   ....

   ....

8. What is my goal for five years? (This is not a wish or a hope. Think *big*.)

   ....

   ....

9. What are my three greatest strengths? (This does not include anything permanent, like aging.)

   ....

   ....

10. What are my three greatest liabilities? (This does not include anything permanent, like aging.)

    ....

    ....

was accompanied by a heavy feeling, like carrying a big rock on my shoulders. That was it. No facts, data, nothing.

I immediately went into guilt and shame over breaking a huge commitment to myself and to those who were supporting this venture. From that, I spent a few days letting it all sink in, asking a few friends for advice. One friend advised me to bike the marathon and suggested that my gut feeling was probably fear or stress. The other friends encouraged me to follow my gut. I reluctantly followed my gut, knowing that disappointment and distance may fall upon those who were supporting me. My other top concern was fear of people wanting data, facts and reasons, and I just didn't have them. I only had my gut instinct!

One day, I planned to visit a friend whose girlfriend just moved to Los Angeles. Her son, Aiden, was visiting and I was anxious to meet him and see their new abode. When I awoke that morning, I had a strong gut instinct not to drive on the highway. I called my friend and told him.

"Hey Bob. I'm really bummed out. I got this strong gut feeling not to drive on the highway, so I'm going to follow that and not visit you today. I'll make it a point to visit with Aiden when he comes to town again, so keep me posted on his next visit."

Here, I shared only my intuition and made a suggestion. No story, data or feeling. Stating my intention was unnecessary and quite obvious.

The very next day, I headed up north toward the poppy fields in Lancaster, and my car broke down on the freeway. Luckily, I safely made my way over four lanes, and a police officer showed up shortly afterwards. He stayed with me for the entire hour while I waited for the tow truck.

INTUITION: THE RITE OF PASSAGE

In my opinion, this is the most important segment in my book. Discerning between "intuition" and "paranoia" is crucial for the grandest self-love and for making the biggest contribution. Most people do not know how to distinguish between the two. Million-dollar deals are made based on gut. There may be left-brained, analytical people out there but, when it comes down to signing on the dotted line, it is often done solely based on gut.

My intuition is my friend.

> When I listen to my inner voice, I make a healthy choice.

> *intuition*—a sense of knowing immediately without reasoning;
> a total knowing, without doubt or internal argument; a reaction
> to a situation not based on knowledge about a person, but
> purely on a gut feeling; a sixth sense; a gut instinct

Listening to my inner voice is about my emotional guidance system intertwined with my values.

- ☼ What messages is my body sending me? What do they feel like? Are they butterflies, fight or flight, projectile vomiting, pins and needles all over or the emotion I have after recalling a dream?
- ☼ Do I have the same familiar feeling I once had in a particular circumstance that went to hell in a hand basket?
- ☼ Do I feel confident and centered? Do I feel strong and willful?
- ☼ Do I feel deflated or ignited in the presence of this person?
- ☼ Might I be actualizing my passions in an unhealthy way?
- ☼ Do I feel respected in the presence of this person?
- ☼ Am I listening with my eyes and heart along with my ears?

PARANOIA

> *paranoia*—delusional fear for oneself; imagination of things or
> responses based on what one thinks they know about a person;
> extreme and irrational fear or distrust of others; a tendency to look
> for hidden meaning behind other people's actions through
> argumentativeness, complaining and low tolerance for criticism

When I am in a place of doubt, is it based on an intuitive hit or am I being paranoid? This is the time to question my values and my truths.

- ☼ Is this the same "feeling" as the one I had in that previous disastrous or victorious situation?
- ☼ What is the most loving choice to make now?
- ☼ Of what about myself am I certain?

This is the time I go within and meditate (be quiet), asking myself these questions and allowing the answers to show up. The answers may be in the form of words through a conversation that has nothing to do with my situa-

> **EXERCISE:**
>
> ## Practical Head or Intuitive Gut?
>
> Choose a situation and answer the following questions. If you have a situation from the past, then act as if you were there when answering the questions. Have fun with it. If it works, use it. If it doesn't, do something different.
>
> 1. In what situation am I that does not intuitively feel right, yet I stay because I am attached to the "juicy feeling" and/or possible outcome of it?
>
> ....
>
> ....
>
> 2. Have I been primarily listening to my practical head or to my intuitive gut?
>
> ....
>
> ....
>
> 3. What would happen if I allowed my gut to lead my head?
>
> ....
>
> ....
>
> *(continued on next page)*

tion, such as a song or a coyote appearing in the middle of the road while I am driving.

At times, I call upon my "red flag raisins" (a "raisin" is *a friend* who *raises the red flag* for me when they see one). We have an open agreement in which they are allowed to lovingly and compassionately share any red flags they see with me. While it is beneficial to surround myself with like-minded people to be my mirror and help me tell myself the truth, only I know my truth . . . no one else.

EXERCISE:
Practical Head or Intuitive Gut? *(continued)*

4. How do I make the greatest contribution right now (regarding this situation)?

....

....

5. What is the highest self-loving choice to make right now?

....

....

6. Am I willing to "JUMP" right now?

....

....

7. How do I feel in this moment?

....

....

∞

Red Flag Raisin Time!

Jenny reconnected with an old colleague, Michael, who came to her for help with an artistic project that literally came through him. Its mission was aligned with her life's work of igniting human potential, and she accepted it with honor. She recalls her entire body filling up with tingles, heat and endorphins. She felt it. She believed in it. She was anchored in the spirit of the project and has held it in her heart and soul every day since then . . . and shall continue to do so. While they continued to write the script, Michael became more courageous in his leadership role.

Fast-forward a few months later: Like a bolt of lightning, they were suddenly attracting a growing number of "light workers" (people who feel inspired to help others through "shining their light," teaching, spiritual meditation, healing, prayer, and writing and speaking with universal love), attaching themselves like bees on honey. Perfect people. Perfect timing ... or so it seemed. The pace with which the project was growing was elating to both of them.

As two more members joined the core group, Jenny questioned Michael's intention in choosing this particular new member named Ellen.

He answered, "She sees things that we do not see."

Jenny knew intuitively that this was not a wise choice but, since Michael was the project creator, she acquiesced. Michael was not hearing her anyway. She noted that his behavior was becoming thwarted; he appeared to be brainwashed.

What was unmistakably occurring felt like paranoia to Jenny as she observed certain behaviors in Ellen, Michael and the others, along with a painstakingly familiar gut feeling. Though she was very excited about and committed to the potential of positively impacting thousands of people, she recalled previous circumstances in her life in which she did not follow her gut instinct. She was not pleased with those outcomes. In order to develop her intuition, she kept this all to herself and made a choice on her own—one that she otherwise would not have made in the past.

Jenny made her choice the moment she realized that her gut feeling was precisely similar to previous unfortunate circumstances. She then asked herself two questions: "How do I make the greatest contribution right now?" (regarding this situation) and "What is the highest self-loving choice to make right now?" She knew the answers with certainty, and relinquished her position on this project.

Feeling victorious, centered, strong and confident, she was elated with trusting herself and her gut instinct more than she ever had. She recognizes that it was the best choice for the good of the whole. She spent four days releasing any hurt or taking things personally, and returned to love for herself and for all of them. She enjoyed watching them go through their own process without wanting or attempting to save them from their potentially unfortunate outcome.

This is their journey, and hers is to make the greatest contribution every day.

JUMP: JOYFUL UNLIMITED MANIFESTING POTENTIAL

When I jump into the unknown, I may experience a myriad of emotions from fear to exhilaration. I think of jumping as a mindset and an approach combined:

> **That moment when my desire surpasses my fear, coupled with precise intuitive action.**

My intuition is my emotional guidance system, like a best friend who supports me in making decisions. I have been in situations where I ignored my gut and the outcome was undesirable. I have also stopped myself from what I desired by using excuses. Every situation has a blessing, yet I encourage my clients to follow and trust their gut.

EMBRACING OUR DIFFERENCES

> *difference*—opposing views; dissimilarity; dispute; controversy; distinction

Consider that my differences may be within myself and not exclusively with others. I may have a conflict going on inside of me if my behavior is incongruent with my personal values. As a human being, I have been created to be different from everyone, yet similar with basic human needs like food, water, love and air.

> If there are two people exactly alike, how boring!

We all have a frame in which we view the world—from family to family, country to country or religion to religion. When I am unwilling to engage in differences with another person, it is usually a position I take of wanting to be right.

In council work, a story is told with many seats in the circle. Each individual shares a personal story on one topic (for example, having an object in the middle and describing what she or he sees). In the end, each opinion is different. The intention of that circle is to reveal that each individual has the privilege to their own opinion, which is not right or wrong, good or bad. It simply is what it is. The gift in differences is to show us that we are either being right about being right or being right about a position that truly supports the intention.

Using the Inside Out Community Arts example, I have witnessed the children's "light bulb" moment when they suddenly realize their commonalities like fear, hope, anger and talent. The bridge is gapped at that moment and harmony abounds. As an artist leader, when I impeccably model the purpose of Inside Out Community Arts, I naturally empower the children to embody that model as well.

HOW TO GET PAST MY DIFFERENCES

If I wait for someone else to be different, I am putting myself in a disempowered position. If I'm about proving that I am "right," then my intentions are misdirected.

To bridge my differences, I:
- Fully express my essense.
- Choose to "agree to disagree."
- Clarify my intention.
- Don't take it personally.
- Honor myself.
- Make a choice for my highest good and the good of others.
- Listen with my ears, eyes and heart.
- Remember that everyone has a soft side.
- Establish stronger boundaries for myself.
- Use self-compassion.
- Enhance creativity, which releases emotions and minimizes fear.
- Remember that I have choice.
- Choose to trust and continue to choose trust again.
- See the child in each person.
- Take a big breath.
- Embrace opportunity and learning by focusing on a goal.
- Detach emotion.
- Be fully present in the moment.

> **EXERCISE:**
> # Getting Past My Differences
>
> Here are some questions you can ask yourself:
>
> 1. Who am I *being* in my differences?
> 2. Am I willing to laugh at myself?
> 3. About what am I choosing to be right?

∞
Unstoppable

Kari is a dear friend and former client of mine. She has cerebral palsy, but you'd never know it by her positive attitude and level of ownership: "Getting good with myself is an ongoing process depending on my role, how I look at it, my resources and my willingness and boundaries that I have set up to live by my values. It's easy to get bogged down in someone else's needs and take on their crap."

At the University of California at Los Angeles, Kari was the coordinator of the Arts and Disability Network for California. When she was in college, she had a friend, Margaret, who was constantly cutting down her talents. Kari thought Margaret was attempting to stop her from living in her greatness. She didn't shake Margaret off because she thought her feelings would be hurt if she heard Kari's truth. Instead of Kari fully expressing herself, she dimmed herself down in the presence of Margaret. *Ouch.*

One day, Kari and Margaret were practicing their German language skills as they were in a German choir. Margaret hissed, "Kari, that sounds kind of hostile!"

Kari had enough of the ridiculous comments and said to Margaret, "Hey, wait a minute! I'm just practicing. What's with the comments? Of course, a foreign language sounds funny coming from my mouth!" Kari laughed at the silliness of Margaret making a big deal and didn't take it personally.

Days later, Kari decided that her truth and full self-expression was most important and said to Margaret, "I think you are consistently snubbing my talents. You have a lot to offer and don't need to project your jealousy on me.

It's clear that you have your own stuff to work on." Kari supported Margaret by giving her "space" through which to work, whatever was going on, while maintaining the positive aspects of their friendship.

Kari continues to apply her commitment to full self-expression in her professional and personal life, which is occasionally not an easy task. "In romance, there are blurred boundaries and, in family, there are a lot of emotions; however, it is always worth being 'Kari with Kari.'" As a result, her productivity has increased, her discipline is engaged and her fears are diminished. She is unstoppable with more lovingness, flexibility, compassion and consideration.

She frequently asks herself, "What are my boundaries in this new situation or relationship?" In her professional life, she says it's easier to set and maintain her boundaries as they are utterly necessary in the flow of information and activity in her workplace. She is realistic in her goal-setting, capabilities and willingness with her people at work. They respect that and delightfully honor her process.

This inspired UCLA to give her a promotion and a raise. Kari enthusiastically accepted but, over time, realized that doing two full-time projects for one full-time position created less productivity, value and quality for those projects. She again assumed the position of "Kari with Kari" and resumed her part-time position (and kept the raise!). As a result, the quality of her work is "unstoppable," which has translated into a renewed commitment of her personal creative projects in writing, editing and publishing.

I'm proud to share that, through a second term of coaching, Kari manifested her dream: to be of service for one year at The Glencree Centre for Peace and Reconciliation (a nonprofit devoted to peace building and reconciliation in Northern and Southern Ireland, Britain and beyond). She recently completed her tenure and is now an English teacher in Frankfurt. *Go Kari!*

TRIGGERS

When I feel triggered (such as a jab in the side, or when my face turns red, my body heats up and my heart races), I know my hot button is hit. It is usually related to a criticism I have of myself. I make it seem real based on my context (I feed it or not).

> The meeting of *two personalities* is like the *contact of two* chemical substances; if there is any *reaction*, both are *transformed*.
> —Carl Jung

I have a choice to feel victimized, which may feel like a benefit, such as:

☼ Being right.

☼ Having an illusion of control.

☼ Using an excuse to take myself out of the game.

I am usually challenged to be present, to stay above the line and in my greatness. How do I desensitize these hot buttons?

☼ I create situations where my hot buttons are frequently hit and practice choosing my reaction. I find a person with whom my triggers are regularly hit and make a fun game out of it.

☼ I stay in the game with full participation. I don't walk away from a relationship just because I feel triggered. It's my stuff, not theirs. I am highly equipped with creativity and humor to make light of the situation in the moment.

POSITION RELEASE

The late Randy Revell, cofounder of Context Associated, was a master at "position release," which means letting go of a conditioned reaction (trigger) in the moment. This trigger, as stated in Triggers teaching, is usually a criticism I have about myself that is now brought to the surface. It is honoring the feeling and emotion, yet not being a victim of it. It is getting clear on my intention in the moment and proceeding with that clear, good intention. It is not taking things personally. It is communicating effectively what is going on for me by voicing my intention and feelings with the willingness to take a breath, walk away, and come back to the conversation or task grounded and clear-headed, full of gratitude instead of anger. I am back in my power (my light). I recommend using the communication model (page 45) when returning to the previously heated conversation.

When I commit to using position release, my entire world changes. My relationships change with myself and with others. Others begin to release their positions, too. As a result, my productivity and confidence go up. Trust and respect improve. Energy and motivation are at play, so my head feels clearer and freer. I now have a bond with the other person(s) that otherwise might not have existed. Trust is strengthened, which leads back to healthier relationships. No worries. Reliability. Faith . . . and back to productivity, energy, motivation . . . an overall sense of well-being.

EXERCISE:
Self-criticism

What things might you have more of if you remove the intensity you've given to your hot buttons?

1. What is one of my hot buttons (such as me thinking about someone else, "You're a micromanaging manipulator!")?

   ....

   ....

2. What do I think about myself (using self-criticism, such as "I'm not valuable")?

   ....

   ....

3. What does my reaction look like (for example, running the story through my head; recapping data to make sure I am "right" about the situation; steaming with anger; dimming down, recoiling or hiding)?

   ....

   ....

4. What attitude might I use to desensitize (such as "I am a powerful human being with a right to make my own decisions")?

   ....

   ....

My wonderful friend, Noel Murphy, and I met in 2001 while he was assisting the "21st Century Leadership" course and I was traveling with Judy and Randy Revell. We became friends instantly and soon realized that we triggered in each other our self-criticism, whereby our conversations became heated and tangled on a frequent basis. We arrived at a point where we wanted to quit our friendship but intuitively knew that was not meant to be, so we came to an agreement.

We created a fun game where we speak up in the moment when one of us was triggered and then we talk it out. In talking it out, we realized from where the trigger was coming and named it with a funny title. In this way, for instance, each time I triggered something in him, he'd stop midstream and say, "Janet, 'it's all about me' is here" or I'd say, "Noel, 'you're wasting my time and not listening' is here." We'd talk it through, but mostly laugh it off and continue our conversation.

∞

I Grow in the Presence of Janet Caliri

by Noel

The first thing I noticed about Janet was her fiery beauty. Back then, I had the thought that she might have a hard time living comfortably with that same beauty. She was actually coming to terms with her magnificent power, and I had a front-row seat.

Here's an example of our interactions: I told her that I had quit singing because I had vocal trouble. She said I didn't have the right to decide that and withhold part of my greatness from the world! I of course began singing again . . . I knew right then that I had entered into "Step Up Even Bigger 101" (and "102" and "103") and had attracted a friend and collaborator for life.

The ensuing outtakes also include challenging what I, at the time, thought was her sense of entitlement. She challenged my self-absorbedness. She set a hard boundary. I edged right up to it and gleamed. I set boundaries with her, too. Eventually, I told her I thought she should be a professional coach because she was so damn smart and had an intuition as sharp as a razor. The day I first met Janet, I went to our mutual mentor, Randy, and told him that I didn't quite know how to handle this new person pressing so many of my buttons. Randy, without missing a beat, told me I should marry her (and he wasn't kidding!).

EXERCISE:
Value Statistic Barometer—Stage 2

In Chapter Two (page 26), you filled out this chart for Stage 1. Now, in the "Stage 2 Date" column, write today's date, and rate yourself again, using a number from "1" to "10" (with "1" being the least and "10" being the greatest level of satisfaction). Ideally, write down the first number that comes to your mind. Rate yourself now *before* you compare these ratings to those of Stage 1. This rating is inclusive of both your personal and your professional life as it is today. These are tangible, measurable results on which to reflect back. Later, in Chapter Eight (page 122), you'll be asked to fill in the same table. You will notice a change when you compare your numbers to Stage 1!

Value Statistic Barometer: Stage 2			
Result	**Stage 1 Date** _____	**Stage 2 Date** _____	**Stage 3 Date** _____
Productivity (energy level, financial gain)			
Accountability/ ownership (using ownership words, keeping my word, owning my results)			
Confidence			
Compassion (for myself and others)			

(continued on next page)

EXERCISE:
Value Statistic Barometer—Stage 2 *(continued)*

Result			
Focus (start, completion, intention, being in the moment)			
Clarity of purpose (Do I know my purpose? Am I on purpose regularly?)			
Commitment (to what I say is most important to me)			
Relationships (to myself and others)			
Communication effectiveness (communication model, intention, listening)			
Balance (Am I doing more of what I love to do?)			

I think we brought up so much in each other that we both knew then that we were kindred catalysts and would play very important roles in each other's lives. We also knew that we would probably hurt each other if we didn't come up with a way to handle all the buttons being hit. Admittedly, the hot-button thing with Janet is barely a blip on the screen compared to all the other ways and levels Janet and I connect and relate and create value together.

Today, we are like family and together we stand for what is possible in the lives of others. I think our current relationship is a finely channeled version of the huge energy she and I evoked in each other. I think she has slain many dragons inside herself and is clearer than ever about her purpose, and so am I. We also have entered into co-leadership and there is no one I'd rather work with and no one easier to adore, and I grow in her presence. I think if you met her, you would, too.

So here is my "I love you, Janet" and my "thank you" for standing for me. You are one of my all-time favorite people and I will always either ride into battle with you or for you. I'll also give up any battle for you . . . or with you, for that matter!

CHAPTER SIX

Purpose

Chapter Five most likely revealed surprises in your level of self-intimacy. Whatever you discovered or did not discover thus far, congratulations on being unstoppable! Remember to embrace everything about yourself. Take your time and enjoy this next chapter. It includes exercises that stretch you from the inside out. Consider inviting your loved ones in discovering your purpose.

> When my desire surpasses my fear, I am living in my potential.

WITHOUT PURPOSE, WHAT'S THE POINT?

> *purpose*—a reason to exist; a desired direction, aspiration, ambition, design goal, or philosophy

On those mornings when I don't want to get out of bed, it is a clue that I am off purpose or am due for a re-ignition. I have a unique purpose here on earth. It is not tangible or a specific vehicle. It is an experience I bring to the world through my contribution.

Perhaps I lost my purpose or I'm uncertain of it. Once I have clarity on my purpose, the veil is lifted and life seems grand. The key is to remain aware of my purpose on a daily basis; otherwise, I get off track or lost, and say "What's the point?"

Falling off track is okay, too. The idea that I am committed to my purpose is more important than beating myself up about falling off track.

EXERCISE:
A Reason to Get Out of Bed

Ask yourself the following questions:

1. For what would I walk over broken glass? About what have I always been passionate?

   ....

   ....

2. To what am I driven in order to do/be/create for the world that I thought/think is missing?

   ....

   ....

3. What is that experience for myself or that I am creating for others? What do I bring to the table?

   ....

   ....

Everything you do has a purpose and you get "juice" out of it. Let's use your current job or voluntary services and determine your purpose by asking yourself the following questions:

4. I took the job and/or volunteer position for a reason. For example, did I take the position for financial security or health benefits? Did I volunteer to network or make new friends? What is it?

   ....

   ....

   (continued on next page)

EXERCISE:
A Reason to Get Out of Bed *(continued)*

5. Are those intentions aligned with what is most important to me?
   ....

6. Am I in a position where I chose to put my desires on the back burner for now (for example, with the purpose of furthering my marriage or caring for an ill relative)? If so, am I living on purpose?
   ....

7. Determine my purpose:

   a. Refer to Question #2 and write down what is missing.
   ....

   b. Refer to Question #3 and write down what I bring to the table.
   ....

   c. Refer to Question #4 and write down my intention for taking the job or volunteer position.
   ....

   d. Choose a title for your purpose by summing up your answers here.
   ....

My life purpose is:
....
....

In high school, I remember breaking up a fist fight between two guys. In my opinion, they were not behaving according to their potential, and I was adamant to show them that there was a way to resolve things other than with the fist. I recall breaking up fights in general, or talking to homeless people on city streets, attempting to create peace among people by revealing their purpose to them.

VEHICLES FOR PURPOSE

What vehicles do I use to express my purpose? Vehicles are *ways* to express and contribute to what I am most passionate about and driven to do.

Here's a simple example: My purpose is igniting human potential. My main vehicle in contributing my purpose is through my coaching. Other vehicles I use include teaching life skills to inner-city youth through performance workshops, hosting family Sunday dinners (potluck dinners for transients), writing this book, photographing, singing and volunteering.

Other examples are by being a parent, a teacher, a lawyer, a painter, an interior designer, a detective, a police officer, a scientist, an accountant, a personal trainer, a gardener, a filmmaker and a chef.

∞

A Well That Never Runs Dry

by Yael

Putting me first didn't happen overnight and it certainly isn't something that I am finished with. I am in the process.

My life has been a succession of doing various projects. I have always been a person who you can come to, and I take care of the situation with success. I always said, "OK, sounds cool, I can do that," and I did it. I value that trait in myself.

I knew I wanted to be an actress and, in my mind, that meant in New York City. I moved there. To me, being an actress was being a person who was a creative, struggling, starving artist in NYC. Then, like in a Hollywood movie, everything would come together and "happily ever after" would occur.

I was fulfilling my idea, yet the struggle within me was that I wasn't enjoying myself. I felt separate from my experience. I wanted the "happily ever after" moment to occur but I didn't realize that the "happily ever after" was the *now in the doing*.

I got myself a job as a flight attendant and flew above it all, as I was going to make money and have time to pursue acting. Yet, I still hadn't redefined for myself what being an actress meant. So, even though I was now living in Los Angeles to make money as an actress, I was doing the same things—I wasn't listening to me. I hadn't accepted my life as it was. I hadn't shifted my perception of thought surrounding my ideas of what I wanted for myself in regard to being an actress, and I wasn't *acting*.

Then, a gift of leaving the airlines came. I took that gift last year. I left flying and the great not-for-profit, and wound down my other teaching gigs. Finally, I stopped *everything*. I mean "head buried under the sand" stopped. I said "no" to more of the same that came my way, felt guilt for a few minutes and eventually took a breath.

Inside my head, I was "yakking" a mile a minute, screaming, *"What do you want?"* over and over again. *Acting* kept coming up for me.

I got a coach and began the process of redefining for myself what being an actress means. I started creating a game plan, yet I still had no instant feedback because I wasn't defining for myself what acting meant to me and for me. I was reacting to "I have to" instead of "I desire.""

Now, it is about redefining and making sure that I am clear. What are my intentions with me and my desires and how do I answer them? You see, I was answering my other ideas without realizing it!

So, the answer to the question "What does putting myself first really mean?" is "Be clear." Know what I am asking. Really know what I am asking, of and for myself, and step into my owning of that. I have the courage to step into my knowing for myself from myself.

For me, putting myself first is about asking, "Is this what I desire? For whom am I doing this? Am I doing this for other people's approval of me or for my own approval?"

This life is filled with so many delicious choices. It is a smorgasbord of opportunity, like a giant buffet. I was feasting on everything. I was working really hard from a place of, "If I do this, it *should* get me that," as opposed to following the desire in the first place, thinking all along, "This will make me better" and "I will learn more, cut my teeth and be a richer and deeper person."

For me, putting myself first doesn't exclude others or commitment. It means turning within and asking myself, "What are the gifts that I have? In what ways will I share with myself? What do I desire to learn and reveal?" Putting myself first has to do with creating a way of being that fills me, even as I draw from myself. I am a well that never runs dry because I am nurturing myself with the process. My practice is where my happiness comes from.

I am grateful that I have the opportunity to choose, ask of myself and give myself the pause to listen instead of react. My approval of me is for me, with center and compassion.

MASTERING MY MOJO

> "Champion of Goodwill"
> —Randy Revell

What is my "mojo"? It is my unique *essence* at my core.

The benefit in mastering my unique essence is to contribute while fully expressing myself. When I fully express who I am, I am positively impacting the human condition. In the world of my mission as a "radiant creative idealist," I am being of service to people to fully express their mojo in a constructive and healthy way. Hence, it is imperative that I am in the process of or have my mojo mastered in order to model that congruently.

Ideally, I am consistently in my mojo and, when I am challenged, I have this information about myself to assist me in "position release" (releasing what I'm holding onto) to embrace differences (see more about this on page 83).

For example, when I am feeling challenged and see no way out, I remind myself of my mojo in order to shift me into a positive attitude.

Here are some examples of mojo titles:
- ☼ Gatekeeper to the freedom of fun
- ☼ Peaceful creator gifting powerful gems
- ☼ Creative conductor of human potential
- ☼ Empathetic visionary for peace
- ☼ Playful teacher for fairness

EXERCISE:
Determine My Mojo

You can determine your essence (your "mojo") and a title for it by asking the questions listed below. Write down as many thoughts and ideas as possible.

1. What penetrates me to such a degree that I'd *walk over broken glass for it*? What am I extremely passionate about?

   ....

   ....

2. What are my top three personality traits? What do my friends and family say to best describe me to someone?

   ....

   ....

3. What are the top five jobs and hobbies I've had throughout my life?

   ....

   ....

4. How have I hurt myself by not being in my mojo, by not being *me* in my light or by not being authentic?

   ....

   ....

(continued on next page)

EXERCISE:
Determine My Mojo *(continued)*

Now, choose a title for your essence by summing up your answers and using the process of elimination to determine what resonates the most.

1. Choose a noun that represents you (refer to your answers to Question #3).

....

....

2. Choose one to two adjectives (refer to your answers to Question #2).

....

....

3. Define your "For what?" (refer to your answers to Question #1 and choose what you most stand for).

....

....

4. Choose a title (use a noun and at least one adjective). You may include your purpose as a tagline but it is not necessary. Make sure the title is compelling (refer to the mojo title examples at the bottom of this page). Say the title out loud, beginning with "I am a/an _____." If you get the chills, you are right on target!

....

....

CORE "JUICY" EXPERIENCES

As a human being, I have two to four primary core inherent needs that I must meet on a regular basis in order to feel fulfilled. These are what I call "juicy experiences" that produce energy and motivation. I meet them constructively or destructively, unconsciously or consciously, in any of these four contexts. I am well served to know these juicy experiences and the vehicle options I have to actualize them. For me, they have been instrumental in healing depression and reducing anxiety.

Examples of my core juicy experiences are discovery, belonging, creative self-expression and intimacy. They are the umbrella to adventure, learning, creativity, nurturing, freedom, contribution and passionate connection.

The best approach to discover these is to list hobbies and vocations I've had throughout the years, starting as early as I can remember. I then asked myself, "What is the juicy experience in this job or in this hobby?"

Some of my *felt experiences* include adventure, excellence, accomplishment, safety, imagination, discovery, fun, harmony, community, fairness, cultivation, control, novelty and the creation of delight. Some of the vehicles in which I actualized these experiences include jobs, hobbies, volunteering, relationships, automobiles, smoking, drinking, shopping, networking and events.

Here are some opportunities I used to meet these juicy experiences *constructively*: singing, gardening, making Sunday dinners, hiking, taking photos, writing, cooking, having a juicy conversation, traveling, coaching, public speaking, facilitating workshops, making healthy friendships, being around dogs, hanging out with my nieces and nephews, saying what's on my mind with compassion and clear intention, using a self-realization process, attending theater and concerts, firing inappropriate clients, doing sales, woodworking and dancing.

I have used the following examples to meet these experiences *destructively*: meeting any of the above experiences without a clear intention, using aggressive behavior in relationships or in the workplace, saying what's on my mind without compassion or clarity of my intention, lashing back at someone, withdrawing from the world, consistently calling in sick, saying "yes" to every invitation and becoming run down, living without boundaries, allowing myself to be micromanaged, underpricing my services, feeling constantly guilty, eating comfort food, ignoring red flags and sucking my thumb.

EXERCISE:
Determine Core Juicy Experiences

Using the table below, make a list of hobbies and jobs, and write down the felt experience for each. When you are done, circle any felt experiences that occurred more than twice. Examples of felt experiences include discovery, autonomy, belonging, safety/security, achievement, adventure, freedom, humor, creative expression and connection. You needn't use my examples; however, please do so if they fit. Do not use examples such as acceptance, love, joy, happiness, satisfaction or success, which are all by-products of the experience.

Add up each felt experience to get your total. Then choose the top two to four experiences to put in your tool box. The three or four with the most repetitions (using the process of elimination) are your top core juicy experiences.

Jobs	Felt Experience

Hobbies	Felt Experience

PURPOSE

∞
Attention, Please!

Jeremy is a perfect example of one who was using the power of thought and actualizing core juicy experiences destructively. He would say, "It's not about me, it's about other people. I'm just a vehicle for hope and possibility." How does this relate to my message of "I'm as good to others to the degree I am with myself"?

I'll share Jeremy's story first and then you can decide. Ten years ago, Jeremy went skydiving and, in an attempt to race his fellow skydiver to the ground, he purposely closed his end cells, ultimately collapsing his entire canopy and plummeting himself to the ground at 120 miles per hour from 1,200 feet.

While Jeremy slipped in and out of a drug-induced coma for one month, his family was told that he would never walk, talk or breathe again on his own. Through his mother's belief in positive thought, she demanded that the doctor leave the room after he said to his medical students, "This is a very sick man!" Thereafter, she requested that the doctors and medical staff, along with his personal visitors, speak only in a positive mindset in his presence.

In his second month of hospitalization, Jeremy was still the guy who loved attention, and was determined to get it constructively or destructively. His mother pointed out that he had a choice to live the role of a victim or look at his situation as an opportunity. A while later, he had an epiphany and realized that his actions and attitude were negatively impacting others and the world.

Jeremy was back in action as a personal trainer and triathlete two and one-half months after the initial injury. From the moment he hit the ground, his mantra was "Everything is okay," and he still uses this thought process on a regular basis. In fact, it is a knowing rather than a wish. He now motivates people through his athletic training and speaking engagements, inspiring them to be good to themselves first so they have more to give to others.

Although Jeremy does, from time to time, slip into old behaviors of being better to others than to himself, he now has a better balance of caring for himself and helping others, and is very "okay" in asking for help!

Jeremy and I have something important in common: He also encourages people to dismiss the nonownership (victim) thoughts and words from their vocabulary. He knows the impact of the power of thought.

The best news is that Jeremy is now walking with a walker! In December 2005, he took his first steps while visiting the Maori Healers in New Zealand. Jeremy is an extraordinary, tangible result for "Me with Me."

MEMORIZE, INTERNALIZE, ACTUALIZE

I suggest memorizing and internalizing your top core juicy experiences as well as you know your name. Any time you want to increase your momentum or productivity—or if you go off track, or feel unmotivated, fearful or negative in any way—tap into at least one of these and actualize it constructively.

It may be as simple as putting your hands in dirt, researching hummingbirds or singing to your favorite music. At the workplace, it may be carpooling with a coworker, having lunch with someone who is positive with which you have something in common or implementing a fun strategy to complete a project. Participating in an appreciation game at the workplace to release stress and agitation goes a long way toward increased productivity and feeling good.

My secret? Knowing that my partner's inherent experiences create a rich and healthy relationship. When I approach it as "my" relationship, I am inclined to assist my partner in actualizing his core experiences constructively on a regular basis. Some readers may be thinking that it's selfish; however, when done from a place of love, respect and admiration, I effectively assist in my partner's happiness!

I believe that the purpose of relationships is to remember who I am and become a higher part of myself. In taking all of the core experiences (for example, belonging, creative self-expression, intimacy and discovery, along with my purpose of igniting human potential), my relationship becomes a healthy vehicle in which to express all of myself from a place of love.

When I adopt the attitude that my partner makes me feel like I belong, or if I wait for him to make me feel a certain way, I am living the role of a victim to some degree. That is a fear-based position, which lacks freedom. Where there is no sense of freedom, there is resistance, resentment and revenge.

I take a moment to think about my work or career. Am I feeling passionate about it or am I staying at my job because I think I have no alternative? If I think I have no alternative, I ask myself, "What experiences fill me up?" If I am a software developer, I may like the experience of producing, discovering, cultivating, being efficient, having security and achieving my goals. Possibilities abound when you decide to actualize these same experiences within your current job or career.

∞
The Passionate Brother, Friend, Father, Son and Husband

My brother Mark was working for the Department of Water and Power in his local town in order to provide for his house, his wife and their two adorable girls. At one point, he was landscaping full time but then chose a full-time job with benefits and maintained his landscaping business on the side. I admire his commitment to security for himself and his family.

For a period of time, Mark was thinking, "This is the only way to provide for my family." However, over time, he was feeling stifled and eventually built up resentment toward his coworkers. Although he was passionate about working in a pleasant and productive environment, he was playing the role of a victim, talking about every one else and their unbecoming behavior, and wanting *them* to change.

I encouraged him to look at himself and see what would happen if he changed his mindset and "reaction" toward them and his environment. This was his first step toward a sense of freedom.

I then suggested that he write down the core juicy experiences in which he felt filled up, and then write beside them the vehicles in which he would actualize them. We both knew that he felt the most fulfilled when he was landscaping and gardening.

In the process of opening up his heart to possibility, Mark attracted a potential landscaping gold mine through a relative of his wife. I brought to his attention that this was not a coincidence but an opportunity through the Law of Attraction to explore. He did.

I'm delighted to share that he acted on his intuition and passion, with clear intention and purpose, and grabbed that gold mine! He is now running a full-time landscaping and design business with several employees. As a result of fully expressing himself, he continues to attract more customers and wakes up more peaceful on a regular basis.

SELF-ACKNOWLEDGEMENT

Self-acknowledgement is like ownership. Perhaps what was modeled for me is to acknowledge other's beauty and gifts but not my own. How does this serve me? Thinking of myself as selfless and modest are two great qualities, I agree. Recalling "I'm as good to others to the degree I am with me" plays a significant role in this conversation. How am I to feel good, motivated and delighted with life and my relationships if I don't take the time to delight in myself? I'm not talking about conceit; I am talking about self-love and respect.

If I model self-love and respect, then I permeate that into my loved ones and the world. Self-criticism does not play a role in the intention of self-acknowledgement. It is healthy to acknowledge my "weaknesses" or "liabilities" and, more importantly, to acknowledge my greatness, so that I am living in that great feeling rather than in the dismal feeling.

As a coach, I direct individuals and teams to make it a daily practice to acknowledge their "wins, victories and accomplishments" so they create a feeling of delight within their bodies and spirits. From this place, they are more productive, positive, healthy and witty. Therefore, they infuse this energy into their workplace and personal relationships.

I suggest having a notebook or journal readily available, taking five minutes each day to acknowledge your "wins," such as:

- ☼ *Emotional:* "I was compassionate with myself in a situation where otherwise I usually am not" (i.e., not taking something personally or not feeling guilty).
- ☼ *Measurable:* "I rode my bike five miles longer than I intended."
- ☼ *Tangible:* "I checked everything off my To Do list today."

Each win is just as important as the other. Some of my clients e-mail me their wins to serve as a mirror for them. As they type, they usually respond with "Hey! I forgot about this . . . this is an excellent accomplishment!"

I begin each coaching session with the client sharing their "wins." This works wonders in bringing them to a place of "Oh, everything *is* okay. I'm much further along and not as unmotivated as I thought."

CREATIVE, FULL SELF-EXPRESSION

I work with a number of clients who are analytical (left-brained). I encourage them to use their right brain (the creative side) consistently to balance the two, since they are inclined to tip the scale toward the left and get out of whack.

I am here to create and, when I suffocate that part of me, I compromise my physical and mental health. I am serious when I say this: I become depressed, anxious, physically impeded, overcontrolling and unsatisfied with my results.

When I was in my twenties, my parents frequently suggested, "Save money for a house," assuming I would want a house, that it was the most important thing to me or that I knew the value of saving money at all. At that

> **EXERCISE:**
> # Who Am I?
>
> 1. My *purpose* in life is:
>
>   ....
>
> 2. My *mojo* is:
>
>   ....
>
> 3. My *core juicy experiences* are:
>
>   ....
>
>   ....
>
>   ....

time, I had no idea of the value of owning property and how it would benefit me in the long run in terms of future financial stability. I always responded to them, "I'm spending my money on creative endeavors because that is what makes me happy. If I allot that money to a home, I'll be in a home all right—a mental institution for not creatively expressing myself!"

That was then and this is now. I look back knowing that they were teaching me the value of money and were really saying that I could have the best of both worlds. Relating to full self-expression, which I think is as equally important as creative self-expression, I also believe that when I stifle that part of me, I compromise my physical and mental health. Full self-expression includes creative expression in addition to communicating opinions, emotions and ideas. When I continue to hold my cards closely, I create a distance that I do not even realize, and suddenly my relationships are not working as well as I'd like and I have poor results.

The communication model is readily available to me as a fun, polite and effective way to fully express myself with respect, dignity, compassion and good intention. There are moments in my life when I just want to break out in song, dance and exhilaration about something that is moving me deeply.

EXERCISE:
Keeping My Word with Ease (Step 2)

The first step of this exercise was done in Chapter Three (page 64). Now, repeat the exercise and use your "core juicy experiences."

1. My core juicy experiences are:

....

....

2. When was a time that I broke my word/commitment?

....

....

3. What was my reason?

....

....

4. Is it true that I made my reason more important than keeping my word?

....

....

5. What do I think would happen if I made my word more important than my reason?

....

....

(continued on next page)

> **EXERCISE:**
> ## Keeping My Word with Ease (Step 2) *(continued)*
>
> 6. How would I feel?
>
> ....
>
> ....
>
> 7. Of what core juicy experience(s) would I be conscious to motivate myself to keep my word and be bigger than my reasons?
>
> ....
>
> ....
>
> 8. When *was* I in touch with a core juicy experience(s) such that I kept my word and was bigger than my reasons?
>
> ....
>
> ....

There is a high price and a blessing in being part of an Irish and Sicilian family from Boston. I may be stereotyped as intense, passionate, full of vigor, guilt-ridden, controlling and shameful—along with being boat loads of fun. I see the gift in all of the descriptions. I really appreciate the times when we just let go and have fun partying, dancing and conversing. I feel safe in this party existence.

There are times when I have kept my mouth shut for fear of the other person being hurt or offended or reacting in a manner that seems unbearable. There is safety in this stifled existence. What serves me and my relationships the most?

If my family and I had the similar communication skills and values, would I feel safe, like I had permission to fully express myself? Yes. Would I feel closer as a family unit? Yes. There is nothing wrong with me or my family today as a unit. I enjoy the process of getting to know—even after all these years—my parents, siblings, cousins, nieces, nephews and, of course, myself.

ME WITH ME

I relish in the idea of each family member releasing their resistance to something they've held onto for the betterment of the quality of their life. To me, this is a beautiful act of self-love.

CHAPTER SEVEN

Evolution

In Chapter Six, what did you come up with for your purpose, mojo and core juicy experiences? Are you still tweaking? Did you get the chills? Remember: for best results, memorize, internalize and actualize! These tools are paramount in anchoring every day. Take the time to give to yourself first and declare who you are at your core.

This chapter uncovers the possibilities of enjoying evolution. Evolution is inevitable. It is a "what is" and you'll discover how to accept "what is" with grace, compassion and dignity.

MOMENTUM

"Evolution" is a process of gradual unfolding, formation, growth, and development into a better me.

> The constant anchor for healthy habits.

The natural human condition is to strengthen goodwill. In order to do so successfully, I am required to get good and stay good with myself first. This usually takes place on January 1st through my resolutions, which typically last about one to three months.

"Why does this occur?" I ask.

Well, as a human being, I am programmed and conditioned a certain way (perfect and beautiful); however; it's the programming that pulls me back to my usual habits and attitudes. I let life intrude, lose focus on what is most important to me, or tell myself that, because of what happened in the past, I cannot (fill in the blank), so what's the point in committing?

Therefore, *re*programming myself takes a bit of time and enthusiastic commitment through repetitive application of new tools acquired through the coaching process. The coaching process is simply self-realization (consciousness) based on, "The more I know about *me*, the more information I have to use constructively."

The good news is that I already have the information and answers, yet most of it is deeply stored in my subconscious. Through self-realization, I easily access that information and use it to create the results that are most important to me; the success rate is very high from the repetitive process. Remember: Doing the same thing over and over again *is* going to produce the *same* result! Therefore, if I want a different result *now*, then I *do* something differently.

> THINK differently.
> BELIEVE differently.
> ACT differently.
> SEE the world through a different observation deck.

What does "do something" mean? First and foremost, there is no failure. When I am open to making an effort—a baby step—I am less likely to be paralyzed with fear, doubt and confusion. To "do something" is to take action on any one thing (for example, water my plants, walk outside for five minutes, lie down and stretch my legs, turn on my favorite music, write my To Do list or knit).

It does not mean using my avoidance techniques (like reading a book, watching TV, eating for the sake of eating or choosing a habit to which I turn for escapism).

These changes will last a *lifetime*, not just a few months or a year.

This progress requires a bit of faith in the unknown and a willingness to experiment, thus I am never locked into anything and always have choice in every moment. Resolutions work temporarily but a new lifestyle works permanently, even if I fall off track. I now have the tools to get back on almost effortlessly.

Growth is not often easy or quickly actualized, yet it holds a greater sense of freedom when I am *fully* committed to it. On the contrary, when I have one foot in and one foot out, I am holding onto my past. I cling to it like a blanket because I have no proof or certainty of future results.

Yet, the only way to feel certain to some degree is to gather knowledge, information and facts, and then take action and see how life unfolds. Yes, this takes faith on my part. One guarantee is that my results will be "different" by way of releasing my past and implementing new attitudes and approaches. When I repeat the same behavior over and over, and expect a different result, I'm setting myself up for disappointment.

I am not dismissing my past as meaningless. I am honoring it as a gift that has molded me into the beautiful human being I am today! I have the choice to take with me bits and pieces that work well and throw away the rest. I have choice in every given moment to rejuvenate and recommit, removing that heavy load I've carried around all these years. Alas, there is space for more energy and productivity as a source to strengthen my momentum and carry me through a magical year and lifetime.

FORGIVENESS

> *forgive*—**pardon; absolve; grant pardon for; cease to resent; remit end of blame; acquit; have mercy; overlook**

When I forgive myself, another or a situation, I am actually creating freedom within myself. So long as I hold onto resentment and forgo forgiveness, I am holding onto exactly that: resentment. I live in the victim role because I have given my power to that person or situation.

Why would I hold all of that negative energy inside? Because I may think that, if I forgive, I am losing my power and will be hurt once again.

I say the opposite: When I forgive, I am taking back my power by letting go and surrendering. Now I am closer to feeling harmonious within myself and with others.

Knowing my boundaries (my values and limits) and staying true to them is important in the success of forgiveness. Without honoring my boundaries, I am likely to feel hurt again.

Once I forgive, I am helping others to forgive and move forward.

∞

Simply Committing to Forgive

A friend of mine was training with a teacher whom she thought was snobby and belittling toward her. She knew this was not ideal for the environment and decided to speak with her about this and clear the air. Before she had the chance, she ran into this teacher at a Sunday service who approached her very differently—with love, praise and no judgment on her face!

My friend soon realized that simply committing to forgive and create a harmonious relationship with her worked on its own without ever having to communicate verbally.

They are now working on some creative projects in the educational system and there is no tension or feelings of belittlement anymore.

ANTIDOTES FOR SUCCESSFUL FORGIVENESS

Usually, when I am reluctant to forgive another, I am reluctant to forgive that same thing inside of me.

Here are a few antidotes to forgive myself and others:
- ☼ Commit to forgiving.
- ☼ Write a letter and never send it.
- ☼ Write a letter and send it.
- ☼ Tell a person I forgive them and myself (have accountability).
- ☼ Spend five minutes (in the shower, driving or exercising) every day, working toward forgiving that person(s) or myself.
- ☼ Focus on what I love most about myself and that person.
- ☼ Use compassion. Remember that I am human and I sometimes make unwise choices. If I continue to make unwise choices, they probably, in those moments, appear to be most important regardless of the consequences. One day I'll get it!

∞

Thoughts on Forgiveness
by Camille

When Janet first asked if I would write a page or two on forgiveness, I was both intimidated and excited. "Forgiveness" is an all-encompassing word!

I mentioned it to a dear friend over lunch and she commented that she had trouble with the way we talk about forgiveness these days because to her, it means one is *condoning a person's behavior*.

I said that is not at all what I think of as forgiveness. I think forgiveness isn't about condoning the offense but about letting go of the anger, rage and pain inside of us.

She mentioned that, in the Jewish tradition, if one does not want to forgive, they must nevertheless give forgiveness if the offender asks three times and makes it clear that they mean to change their ways. What a profound concept!

Curiously, when I got home, I looked up "forgive" in several dictionaries: "to give up resentment of or claim requital for insult; to grant relief from payment of; to excuse for a fault or an offense; pardon; to renounce anger or resentment against." I was surprised by what I had heard and read. It never occurred to me that forgiveness can mean so many different things to people. What follows is the first step regarding *what forgiveness means to me*.

To forgive doesn't mean that I finally decide I'm OK with the offense, but rather that I am ready and willing to let go of the feelings inside that weigh me down and hold me back from wholeness. If someone did harm to another, even killed a person, I don't think I could forgive them in the sense of absolving them from what they did. If this person is a danger to others, they need to be held in protective custody in some manner and, if possible, be guided to live their lives differently.

It is not in my power to make the offender become someone else, however. I need not approve of the behavior, but it is within my power to experience love for all mankind beyond their behavior.

When I worked at Patton State Hospital for the Criminally Insane, people used to say, "How can you work with those people? They're murderers," etc. However, when I get there and hear their stories, or see the inner child who obviously never had a chance to reveal her/himself in a creative workshop, I'd realize that the spirit of this human being has been horribly damaged.

Nonetheless, there is a light that abides in them as in all of us. This person needs to be institutionalized quite probably for the rest of their physical life, but can I find some inkling of love for them? We say we are all one. If I reject them, I am rejecting a part of my divine connectedness.

At the same time, in forgiving another, I believe I must not have expectations that the other will necessarily change or even outwardly respond to the forgiveness. That is no small thing to practice. I remember when I gave a gift to someone and they gave it to someone else, I was so upset! However, if I have truly let it go to them, then it is theirs—to do with as they please. The gift no longer belongs to me.

In the same way, to forgive is "to give" my forgiveness freely, without expectations or conditions. It comes from me. It is about my willingness/desire/need to give the gift. Where it goes from there is beyond my reach.

Forgiveness begins with me. I need to forgive myself for not making things turn out differently. I'm entitled to the full range of my feelings in response to an offense, but I need to forgive myself for holding onto my rage and desire for revenge. I need to forgive myself for letting my thoughts and feelings keep me from being in this moment and the next moment. I'm not sure how I can truly forgive another until I've forgiven myself.

In speaking of the Kosovo conflict in 1996, I heard radio commentator Dave Ross say: "Forgiveness is letting go of all hope for a better past." This is one of my mantras. My process used to begin with, "Why? Why? Why?!" Eventually, I'd realize that nothing I can do or say will ever make the past different and I'd say, "I can do nothing about this! I'm powerless to change this person's action. It already happened and it's over!" I would finally rest my weary mind and ask myself, "What now?" Now, I mostly *begin* with "What now?"

There is an African proverb, which *Thich Nhat Hanh* also refers to "An enemy is one whose story we have not heard." Another of my mantras! It doesn't say it hasn't been *told* but rather *heard*. Until we are willing to hear the story of the other (and, in many cases, that person doesn't really know, much less is ready, to tell their story), we are destined to continue the cycle of violence and revenge, whether it's physical, emotional or spiritual.

Not forgiving hurts me. It makes my body, my spirit and my heart sick. It makes it hard to find love because my heart is not really open or ready for intimacy. Until I choose to find some acceptance of my life as it is, rather than how I wanted it to be, I wound me. If I choose to let go of a better past; if I choose to "give up resentment of or claim to requital"; if I choose to forgive myself and pardon the actor, not the action—then I believe there is room, nay boundless space, for new life in the remainder of my days.

∞

Blue Line–Green Line Greed

In 1992, just after returning from a yearlong stint in "Up With People" (a nonprofit, nonreligious, educational, and musical organization bridging the gap between social differences), my dear friend Roberto came to visit me in Boston. At that time, I did not have a car and enjoyed the train for transportation.

After "dropping" Roberto off at the airport, I took the train's blue line to the green line on that fateful Friday night. Standing on the platform, waiting for my train, I *felt* something goin' down. I remember a cluster of boys, in their late teens or early twenties, circling up and snickering in whispers, heads turning and nodding. As quick as lightning, I heard a *bang* and found myself hiding behind a concrete pillar . . . and then there was a resounding silence.

I slowly got up and looked around. Silence. Stillness. People flat on the ground, curled into balls, scattered everywhere. As a medical professional, I intuitively tiptoed toward the open platform where I found a man lying on his stomach. He was alive; his two friends appeared frightened by their realization that their friend, Brian, was injured. I was surprisingly joined by an enthusiastic helper, and we slowly turned Brian on his back, raising his head on a pizza box. My new "helper" put on his latex gloves and we went to work.

I will always remember looking up and seeing Brian's two friends weeping in hysterics. "Will he live? Is he going to be okay? We're on a business trip from California and decided to stay one day longer for sightseeing."

I thought, "*Why*? Why did you stay *one* more day to sightsee?"

The paramedics took 40 long minutes to arrive and, long before that, our medical skills were exhausted. There was only so much we could do for a man who caught a ricochet bullet to his liver.

I took the train home, feeling scared, numb, helpless and worthless. I turned on the TV news to discover that Brian died on the way to the hospital. Tears welled up in my eyes and ears, thoughts collided in my head like bumper cars and I felt like a deflated balloon. My ego came into play: "I could have saved him! I could have been the one to the rescue!"

A fellow radiologist suggested that I see a therapist to work through this trauma. Still in denial, I declined. It wasn't until 10 years later that I realized I had not forgiven myself or those boys who pulled the trigger for a stupid leather jacket worn by an innocent kid waiting for the blue line.

CHAPTER EIGHT

Review

Are you on the path to forgiveness? It's an excellent start towards your growth, peace of mind and potential. Remember that everything is temporary. Breathe. You've also heard some strong opinions about forgiveness and taking action, with which you may or may not agree. Again, there is no right or wrong, good or bad—only your truth and what feels proper for you.

Congratulations on remembering who you are at your core. Kudos to you for experimenting with the teachings, working the exercises and taking a very good look at the new results in your life. You are courageous. You have the choice to go back to each chapter that you think is unfinished and rediscover who you are at any given moment, because you have choice!

This chapter is a recap of your results and the ensuing steps for momentum, sustainability and productivity of the shiny new you!

NEW RESULTS

By now, I am well on my way to creating what is most important to me.
- ☼ My productivity, confidence and level of ownership are elevated.
- ☼ My relationships and communication effectiveness are stronger.
- ☼ I am more compassionate with myself and others.
- ☼ I have created more balance in my life by building the "being in the moment" muscle and doing more of what I love to do.
- ☼ Overall, my frame on life is different because it has fewer layers of past opinions, judgments and attitudes.
- ☼ I now take the position that "my thoughts, feelings and results are mine" and "I have choice in every moment."

- ☼ I tend to quickly relinquish triggers that I used to hold onto for days, weeks and months.
- ☼ I laugh at myself more often and take life less seriously.
- ☼ Deep gratitude for everything—whether I judge it to be negative or positive—is prominent in my daily life.
- ☼ Courage regularly surpasses fear.
- ☼ Full self-expression assumes the position; squelching takes a back seat.
- ☼ Juicy experiences have a whole new healthy meaning now.
- ☼ Waking up every day with purpose is an unfamiliar, yet welcomed, experience.
- ☼ Freedom is a newfound, consistent feeling inside.
- ☼ Most importantly, I have fallen in love with myself more deeply.

SURROUNDING MYSELF WITH LIKE-MINDED PEOPLE

I've been blessed with attracting extraordinary, eclectic, open-minded and creative people. I've also been equally blessed with attracting chaotic, toxic, depressive and negative people. They've all been wonderful mirrors for me to remind me of who I am.

Nevertheless, it is unnecessary to continually attract the "dazzle" (destructive drama) to learn my lessons. This is when I harness ownership, self-respect, intuition, compassion, empathy and forgiveness to say "thank you and so long" to the dazzle.

I choose to surround myself with like-minded people. Whatever "like mind" (similar tastes) means to me, define that and commit to being around the people who embody that. In any case, I am worthy of having a community of people who are devoted cheerleaders, adulators, admirers and promoters of my mojo.

As the saying goes, "Birds of a feather flock together." Every autumn, birds fly in splendid formation with perfect communication and confidence in each other in the group. Consequently, they are equipped to suddenly change direction and move in perfect harmony to avoid danger.

LEADERSHIP SUPPORT

I think it's interesting that the English dictionary does not use the word "change" or "value" in any definition of "lead," "leader" or "leadership."

My definition of a "leader" is someone who is willing "to create change that creates value." The one who is in charge of or in command of others is there to create invaluable changes when necessary. The leader possesses integrity, innovation, trustworthiness and respect, thus inspiring others to follow.

Who do I know who exemplifies these traits? Is it me? Perhaps I am a leader in some area of my life and surround myself with those of like mind. If not, isn't now the time to make that happen?

When I moved to Los Angeles, I knew no one. I quickly gathered alliances and, after four months, I created a free monthly Leadership Circle with the intention of igniting others *and* surrounding myself with those who would support me in growing . . . a solid foundation of leaders. The group continued to grow, even while some dropped out, and it eventually took on a life of its own. While I no longer lead it today, it continues to bring value to a consistent assembly of people.

As I shared in the preface of this book, when I moved to San Francisco, I was immediately blessed with leaders who were sincerely committed to my growth and joy . . . and, from there, spawned an entire community with the same unfailing values.

I am not suggesting that I dismiss my family or those whom I love. I frequently remind myself to play it big, shine my light and live on purpose. This may require me to invite more people into my life and/or reassess my existing relationships.

I know who the enlightened are by how I feel when I am around them, how the sound of their voice is anchored as they share their values and aspirations and the undeniable life in their eyes.

POTENTIAL

I believe in your potential until you do. *I do!* I always have, from the time I remember as far back as I can remember. Like a mystic, I know the part of you that is unrevealed. I see through you and hear behind what you are saying.

Take a deep breath. Read to yourself:

Even though there are times when I forget my own potential, I am quietly reminded of it through my relationships, both personal and professional, and I am grateful for that.

I've had the experience of people being intimidated around me, and they go away without explanation. I have finally resolved this within myself and accept it fully. My life is that much richer.

REVIEW

My burning desire is to know, accept and live in my potential, my possibility of manifesting and being anything I desire, because I am an unlimited, inherently able and capable being.

I do my best to always live from this perspective.

When my desire surpasses my fear, I am living in my potential. I pay no mind to what others say or think, or how the "market" is doing. I live my life to its fullest in the midst of the failing real estate, stock and job markets; oil market turbulence; company closures; presidential election; and, of course, the wars in the Middle East.

Throughout this book, I have gained insight and invaluable techniques for living in my potential—safely, respectfully, peacefully and with joy.

I deserve to live in my potential: a life full of joy, love, peace and light. No one has the right to attempt to seize or stifle me from living in my full essence.

Remember: No one can control me or stifle that without my permission. It's my choice that frees me from victim mentality (outer chaos) and reverts me back to ownership.

What's on the inside shows up on the outside.

It's time to take the "after" photo of yourself today. Place it in the "Completion Date" box on page 25.

EXERCISE:
Value Statistic Barometer—Stage 3

In Chapter Two (page 26), you filled out this chart for Stage 1; in Chapter Five (page 90), you filled it out again for Stage 2. Now, in the "Stage 3 Date" column, write today's date. Rate yourself again, using a number from "1" to "10" (with "1" being the least and "10" being the greatest level of satisfaction). Rate yourself now *before* you compare your answers to Stages 2 and 1. Ideally, write down the first number that comes to your mind. This rating is inclusive of both your personal and your professional life as it is today. These are tangible, measurable results on which to reflect back. Compare your rating to Stage 2 and then to Stage 1. Notice the change!

Value Statistic Barometer: Stage 3			
Result	Stage 1 Date _____	Stage 2 Date _____	Stage 3 Date _____
Productivity (energy level, financial gain)			
Accountability/ownership (using ownership words, keeping my word, owning my results)			
Confidence			
Compassion (for myself and others)			
Focus (start, completion, intention, being in the moment)			

(continued on next page)

EXERCISE:
Value Statistic Barometer—Stage 3 *(continued)*

Result			
Clarity of purpose (Do I know my purpose? Am I on purpose regularly?)			
Commitment (to what I say is most important to me)			
Relationships (to myself and others)			
Communication effectiveness (communication model, intention, listening)			
Balance (Am I doing more of what I love to do?)			

APPENDIX A

Coaching Services and Information

☼ **Individual & Executive Coaching**
One-on-one sessions. Unlimited e-mail access and sequential photography. *Free* preliminary assessment.

☼ **Workshops**
Experiential leadership workshops for professional and/or personal development. Janet truly enjoys interacting with a group of people where she creates a fun and confidential environment enriched with laughter, connection and a shift in perspective.

☼ **21 Days to Yes!**
Your life *is* the workshop!

Janet's 21-day program, "21 Days to Yes!" is developed based on proven studies that it takes 21 days to make or break a habit. ("Habit" in this case may be a conscious or unconscious pattern, mindset or context.) She has personally experienced this 21-day phenomenon and, through working together, her clients have produced great results using the techniques and ideas she teaches.

☼ **Me with Me**
A 12-week practicum based on *Me with Me.* Step into your potential one step at a time. Unlimited e-mail and *free* workbook included.

COACHING SERVICES AND INFORMATION

☼ **Ownership Editing**

There is magnificent power in the *word* and *thought*. Did you know that certain verbal inflections and grammatical categories make or break a deal in the sales and marketing world?

Choosing first person versus second or future tense versus present has a huge impact on a potential client saying "yes" or "no." Are you aware of the key words that discard confidence and generate a feeling of resistance? Come see an example and start creating powerful content for extraordinary results.

☼ **Speaking Engagements**

Are you a company or organization committed to your potential? Would you like to instill the secrets to ease and freedom, productivity and balance at the workplace? Using eight simple steps, Janet has a fun and thought-provoking *oxygen-mask* methodology for you to immediately instill in your workplace, creating results that are important to you.

☼ **BBS Radio Talk Show Host and Life Coach**

55 minutes of *free* coaching through live conversation.
Check www.bbsradio.com/sightforsound for details.

APPENDIX B

Links for More Information

www.sightforsound.com
Janet Caliri's coaching website

www.bbsradio.com/sightforsound
Janet Caliri's free coaching radio show

www.linkedin.com/in/sightforsound
Networking tool

www.selfgrowth.com/experts/janet_caliri.html
Expert teachings and products

www.extraordinarylearning.com
Home of 21st Century Leadership

www.contextassociated.com
Leadership company

www.insideoutca.org
Inside Out gives youth from all backgrounds the tools, confidence and inspiration to make a positive difference in their communities and the world ... from the inside out.

LINKS FOR MORE INFORMATION

www.upwithpeople.org
Up With People sparks people to action in meeting the needs of their communities, countries and the world while building bridges of understanding as a foundation for world peace.

www.craigslist.org
A central network of on-line communities featuring
free, classified advertisements for jobs, internships,
housing, personals, services, community and forums
on various topics

www.agapelive.com
An international center that stands for love, peace and being a beneficial presence on the planet

http://en.wikipedia.org/wiki/Carl_Jung
Carl Jung was a Swiss psychiatrist, an influential thinker and the founder of analytical psychology.

www.nealedonaldwalsch.com
Author of "Conversations with God" series.

Glossary

Note: These definitions are my own and align with their use in this book.

Able: having *inherent* adequate functionality for doing or being something; therefore, being "unable" is impossible

Accountable: being the source of and responding to my results, choices and actions

Against: opposed to; anti; adverse to; attracting that which I oppose rather than what I desire or stand for; "what I resist persists" ("what I resist" is the same as "what I am against or do not want" and I always get what I focus on!)

Because: for the reason that; due to the fact that; an excuse to do the same thing over and over again so I am *not* responsible for it

But: a throwaway word that discards what was just communicated

Can: having *inherent* ability, function, power or skill

Can't: implies inability, lack of choice and ownership

Choice: election; option; preference; selection; alternative. Choice is always available to me in any given moment. Making a choice may be in an outward action or an internal perception shift.

Chronic fatigue syndrome: disorder characterized by debilitating fatigue and a combination of flu-like symptoms such as sore throat, swollen lymph glands, low-grade fever, headaches and muscle pain or weakness

Codependency: when one person is physically or psychologically dependent on another in an unhealthy way

GLOSSARY

Communication effectiveness: adequate, efficient and productive exchange of ideas by writing, speaking, listening or using signals with a desired result

Communication model:
Intention (purpose, what for)
Data (facts, five senses)
Story (interpretation, perception)
Feeling (emotion)
Suggestion (idea, follow through)

Compassionate: kind, merciful, soft and tender; having an understanding acceptance of human behavior in myself and others

Congruence: quality or state of agreeing or corresponding; agreement; harmony; conformity; integrity

Consequence: result that is not necessarily deemed as bad, negative, poor, unsatisfactory or unfavorable, but simply the effect, result or outcome of something occurring earlier

Conscious: opposite of "unconscious"; aware of one's own existence, sensations, thoughts and surroundings; sensitive to something; cognizant

Constructive: opposite of "destructive"; productive; useful; handy; healthy

Context Associated: leadership and personal development company once based in San Francisco (now in Seattle) and founded in the 1970s by Judy and Randy Revell

Craigslist: a central network of on-line communities featuring free, classified advertisements for jobs, internships, housing, personals, services, community and forums on various topics

Degenerative disk disease: degeneration of the intervertebral disk, when the disks in between the spine vertebrae dehydrate, or dry out, and lose their function to act as shock absorbers

Depression: low state of vital powers or functional activity; may be caused by chronically being a victim of circumstance, including thoughts, emotions and physical body

Destructive: opposite of "constructive"; unproductive, unhealthy, unfavorable or adverse

Detached: not attached to an outcome or result; feeling empowered, capable and independent

Difference: disagreement or controversy; antagonistic, unharmonious conflict

Discipline: activity, exercise or regimen that develops or improves a skill; training

Don't: opposite of "do"; negating (resistant) message to the subconscious mind, which attracts and manifests nothing

Emotional guidance system: intuition; scale of emotions—from joy to fear—letting me know when I'm in the process of attracting and creating what I do and do not desire

Enlightenment: state of full comprehension; illumination; nirvana; revelation; understanding; wisdom

Entitled: thinking that I have a right to something without earning it

Epiphany: sudden, intuitive perception of or insight into the reality or essential meaning of something; moment when the light bulb goes off!

Epstein-Barr virus: type of herpes virus that causes infectious mononucleosis

Externalize: attribute to outside causes; look outside of myself; have a victim mentality

Faith: belief without any evidence

Gratitude: appreciation; thankfulness for what is, even if I do not see it

Have to: obligated to; being without choice; experiencing a feeling that conjures up resistance, resentment and guilt; putting others before myself or dishonoring what feels best for me

Hot button: slang for "trigger"; stimulus that initiates or precipitates one or a series of reactions

Ho'oponopono: ancient problem-solving art from the Hawaiian culture, which teaches that life in fact can be easy; to make right or to rectify an error by connecting with divinity. Repeat silently over and over: "I'm sorry. Please forgive me (for whatever is going on inside of me that is causing this). I love you. Thank you."

Hostel: inexpensive, supervised lodging place for young travelers

Inside Out Community Arts: Through the arts, Inside Out Community Arts promotes healthy interaction among diverse, at-risk and underserved Los

Angeles middle-school youth. Led by specially trained teams of professional artists and high-school age mentors, Inside Out bridges cultural, geographic, socioeconomic and differently abled boundaries to support youth in creating and presenting topical theater and art, empowering them to make positive choices as individuals and members of the greater community.

Insomnia: persistent difficulty falling asleep or staying asleep despite the opportunity

Integrity: congruency; being who I say I am; completeness; entirety; honesty; soundness of moral character or wholeness; absoluteness; totality; honor; uprightness; purity; virtue

Intention: direction; ambition; destiny; purpose

Internalizing: taking in and making an integral part of one's attitudes or beliefs

Intuition: sense of knowing immediately without reasoning; gut instinct

Judging function: ability to act or decide based on an opinion, estimate, calculation or evaluation by means of thinking and feeling

Judgment: ability to make up a story, opinion or perception of a person, place or thing based on data from the five senses; not necessarily negative and not necessarily true in the eye of the beholder. A judgment can be "positive" ("I see the gray sky and it is a beautiful day!"). When a judgment is "negative," we have choice *not* to act on that judgment. I believe judgment has a bad and negative rap due to most people *acting* on that judgment and first impressions, and not giving it another chance ("She never returns my calls, so I think she doesn't care about me" or "She is a flake").

Juicy experience: sensation of being, emotion and consciousness

JUMP (Joyful Unlimited Manifesting Potential): jumping into the unknown; taking a risk; advancing rapidly from one level to another

Law of Attraction: I make real that to which I put my attention; like attracts like; what I focus on, I get

Liability: something disadvantageous, detrimental, harmful or unfavorable; something that holds me back

Lupus: chronic autoimmune disease when the immune system attacks the body's cells and tissue, resulting in inflammation and tissue damage in the heart, joints, skin, lungs, blood vessels, liver, kidneys and nervous system

"Makes me": thinking that something or someone is making me feel, do or think a certain way (even if I judge it positively). Statements such as "She makes me mad," "The rain makes me sad" and "He makes me feel beautiful" come from a victim mentality because the speaker thinks the outside source is making them be/think/feel a certain way.

Manifestation: materialized form; indication of the existence, reality or presence of something

Maori Healers: From the native Polynesian population of New Zealand, the ancient Maori art of healing is passed down to selected family members from generation to generation. It consists of Romiromi (bodywork) and Mirimiri (counseling) cultural therapy, which creates harmony and balance in the body. It is a communal process where there may be one, two or more healers working on one client or several clients at the same time in the same room

Measurable: has a quantifiable degree, proportion or dimension; is able to estimate the relative value by comparison with some standard

Mindset: thought processes of an individual or group; fixed mental attitude, psyche, disposition and outlook on life; the frame through which I view the world

Need: lack of something wanted or deemed necessary; obligation to; externalization

Nonattachment: opposite of "codependency"; a way to rid my life of unnecessary unhappiness by disengaging, dissociating or removing; conditioned feeling of being closely tied to a person, thing, cause, ideal or the like

Perceiving function: awareness, knowledge or identification gained by the senses using sensation or intuition

Position release: act of letting go of a conditioned reaction (trigger) in the moment

Potential: state of being or becoming; unlimited possibility; unlimited outward expression; inherent capacity for growth or development

GLOSSARY

Power behind the throne: quiet catalyst; inspiration for others; encourager; prompter; provoker; igniter of potential

Productivity: increase in energy; catalyst for tangible and measurable results; quality of producing readily or abundantly; fertility

Purpose: contribution and actualization of an *experience* for the reason for which something exists

Reaction: action in response to an opposed opinion

Reason: basis or motive for an action, decision or conviction; declaration made to explain or justify an action, decision or conviction; crutch for doing the same thing over and over again without having to take responsibility for it

Red Flag Raisin: person who raises the red flag (a "warning sign") for me when they see one

Reprogramming: programming again; reversing the cause of absorbing or incorporating automatic responses, attitudes or conditioning

Right: choice or action that is advantageous, appropriate, favorable, healthy, true or wise for me; not necessarily for or about another person

Rite of passage: any important act or event that serves to mark a passage from one stage of life to another (in this case, my intuition is the tool used to support me in this passage)

Seasonal affective disorder: mood disorder in which people who have normal mental health throughout most of the year experience depressive symptoms in the winter or, less frequently, in the summer, repeatedly, year after year

Should: have no choice; must; ought to; have a duty to; need to; have a sense of obligation; have resistance, resentment and guilt. When I use "should," I put others before myself or dishonor what feels proper to me.

Shunned: deliberately disregarded; failing to be noticed; ignored; ridiculed

Sorry: conventional apology or expression of regret. "Sorry" is often used to repeat the same behavior over and over again instead of taking responsibility to change it.

Spirituality: quality or state of being spiritual; of or relating to the mind, intellect or soul; intangible; lacking material body, form or substance

Story * Poof! * Action!: When I am concocting a negative *story* about myself, I instantly *dissolve* it and take a simple form of *action* with something I love to do.

Stream-of-consciousness writing: uninhibited writing with pen or pencil

Subconscious: existing or operating in the mind beneath or beyond consciousness; totality of mental processes of which the individual is not aware; psychic activity just below the level of awareness. When a message enters the subconscious mind, it is taken as a true fact and stored for future reference. It does not have reasoning skills and thus does not distinguish "right" from "wrong" or judge the information it receives. For this reason, the strength of subconscious messages has virtually no boundaries, and can thus be unfavorable when used improperly. It has unlimited power.

Supposed to: intended to; had a sense of obligation with internal expectation; noncommittal

Surpass: excel; exceed; outmatch; transcend; go beyond

Tangible: palpable; tactile; touchable

Timeline: committed time by which something is to be completed or commenced

Transformation: internal process of change, reprogramming, metamorphosis, permutation and transmutation

Trigger: stimulus that initiates or precipitates one or a series of reactions

Trust: reliance and confidence on the integrity, strength and surety of myself, a person or a thing

Try: attempt to do or accomplish; test the effect or result of; aim; make an effort; use a fraction of commitment; promote unaccountability

21st Century Leadership: top-notch, one-week experiential leadership and personal development course

Uncharted territory: unknown; event never experienced before; unfamiliar area

Unconscious: opposite of "conscious"; without awareness, sensation or cognition; not perceived at the level of awareness

GLOSSARY

Ungrounded: agitated, uncertain, indecisive, confused and inconclusive; opposite of "solid," "firm," "having a foundation or support" or "rooted"

Unreasonable: not governed by or predicated on reason; beyond normal limits; shocking; going above and beyond one's comfort zone

Vulnerable: willing to be seen, transparent and open to receive; willing to be human

Want: lack; need

Win: achievement; result of which I am proud; not of competition

Wrong: choice or action that is disadvantageous, inappropriate, unfavorable, unhealthy, untrue or unwise for me; not necessarily for or about another person

Yardstick: any standard of measurement or judgment

About the Author

> **Sight for Sound:**
> When I *see* things as they truly are, I make *sound* choices.

THE VISION BEHIND SIGHT FOR SOUND

Janet Caliri is a gifted and intuitive life coach igniting human potential all over the world. She believes that we are all here to contribute; that each and every one of us has a unique gift that lends itself to strengthening the fabric of goodwill; that the first step is to discover who we really are and, as we begin to feel alive and fulfilled, this is the experience to carry us through our mission.

Through a series of conversations and sequential photography (page 25), she teaches people and companies how to get out of their own way and live in their potential—in many cases, exceeding expectations. Her charismatic and approachable personality sets the stage for a professionally fun, confidential and comfortable environment while never falling short of the objective.

Born and raised in the Boston area, Janet has an extensive background in radiology, and graduated in 1996 from the New England School of Photography in Boston. When she combined her love for igniting human potential and knowledge of the photographic medium, Sight for Sound was born.

She credits her success to a mature blend of dedication, creativity and a thirst for growth and refinement. As a result, her coaching practice has helped many individuals, entrepreneurs and organizations take their dreams and visions to the next level.

ABOUT THE AUTHOR

Janet is a field-certified life coach committed to continuing education through participating in leadership training, personal development, and similar studies such as working with inner-city youth and writing a book on the beauty of noses. She is a member of the International Coaching Federation, Independent Writers of Southern California, and an Artist Representative on the Board of Directors at Inside Out Community Arts in Los Angeles.

Notes

NOTES

ME WITH ME

NOTES

ME WITH ME

Made in the USA